# Action Research: Principles and Practice

Related titles from Macmillan Education:

*Teacher Appraisal: a practical guide*
Ted Wragg

*Children Becoming Readers*
Henry Pearson

*Managing for Learning*
John Buckley and David Styan

*The Caring Role of the Primary School*
Editors: Kenneth David and Tony Charlton

*Assessing and Teaching Language: Literacy and Oracy in School*
Mary Neville

*Norwood* was *a difficult school*
Jean Lawrence and Margaret Tucker

*Careers Across the Curriculum*
Catherine Avent OBE

# Action Research: Principles and Practice

**Jean McNiff**

With a foreword by Jack Whitehead,
Lecturer in Education,
University of Bath

MACMILLAN EDUCATION

First published 1988.

Published by
MACMILLAN EDUCATION LTD
Houndmills, Basingstoke, Hampshire RG21 2XS
and London
Companies and representatives
throughout the world

Printed in Hong Kong

British Library Cataloguing in Publication Data
McNiff, Jean
Action research: principles and practice.
1. Action research. Methodology
I. Title
300'.72
ISBN 0-333-45318-2

# Contents

# Acknowledgements

I am grateful to David Rees of Kingsleigh School for his careful review of the manuscript, and to Peter Mann, Chief Adviser in Dorset, for his painstaking work which contributed much to the text.

Professor John Elliott has been most helpful in providing information about the Cambridge Action Research Network and similar ventures. My thanks to him.

I am grateful to Martin Forrest, Margaret Foy, Zita Gisborne, Mike Parr, Sue Kilminster and Carol Smith for their generous permission to use their material in the book. Thanks also are due to Maureen Barrett, joint coordinator of the course 'Supporting teachers in their classroom research', for permission to acknowledge her part in the project. Her inspiration has given rise to the rich material which appears in the case studies.

John Aldridge and Miranda Carter, my publishers at Macmillan Education, have always been a constant source of encouragement.

I acknowledge with gratitude permission to use copyright material on p. 77 from David Hopkins, *A Teacher's Guide to Classroom Research* (Open University Press, 1985). Illustrations are reproduced by kind permission of the following: Fig. 3.3 (Deakin University); Fig. 3.4 (John Elliott); Fig. 3.5 (Dave Ebbutt).

I am grateful to Joan Whitehead and Ronald King for their support at critical moments, and particularly to Denis Vincent of the North East London Polytechnic for his several commentaries on the manuscript. His contribution has been instrumental in producing the better parts of the book.

Thank you to my good friend Alan Hyde for his patience in many long hours of listening while I talked through the project.

And finally, Jack, my friend and teacher, who was always there to advise on the manuscript, and who started it all in the first place.

# Foreword

***Jack Whitehead***

School of Education, University of Bath

Whatever we might think of the influence of the government's policies for the national curriculum, testing and privatisation, on schooling, we are faced with the certainty that improvements in the quality of education are dependent upon the professional competence and high morale of teachers. While in-service support for teachers is crucially important in their professional development there still exists a division between academics, who believe that educational knowledge is to be studied through subjects such as philosophy, psychology, history and sociology, and teachers who believe that educational knowledge is embedded in their competent practice.

The profession now needs a form of support which can unite teachers and academics in a collaborative endeavour to improve education. We must find a way of bridging the traditional divide between educational theory and professional practice. My own view is that we academics have been guilty of sustaining an inappropriate way of thinking about education, a way of thinking which is deeply embedded in an educational theory which is divorced from practice.

Increasing numbers of teachers are gaining the confidence to challenge the way academics have traditionally thought about education. They are developing ways of understanding practice which involves the systematic examination of practical problems. They are imagining solutions, acting and evaluating the outcomes of their actions. These teachers are examining their practice and showing the tension which exists when they feel they are not able to live fully their values in practice. They show their commitment, often over years, to work out ways of improving their practice in terms of their values.

Such case studies often involve visual records on videotape of classroom practice. These tapes enable the teachers to show what they mean when they claim that their educational values can be seen in their practice. This teacher/researcher movement is now well integrated into INSET provision throughout the country and makes an important contribution to professional knowledge. I believe it forms a secure research base for the advancement of the profession into a General Education Council. A question we should tackle in the immediate future is how can we collaborate to institutionalise the teacher/researcher movement into an Educational Council for the support of professional development?

Through its emphasis on critical evaluation of practice within a democratic framework, the action research movement has integrated researchers from different disciplines and curriculum areas who share a concern to improve practice and to understand the process of improving practice. There is a healthy tension in the movement between those whose work emphasises either practical improvement or the understanding of the process. The work of academics in the field certainly emphasises 'understanding', but is weak on case studies of their own attempts to improve practically a process of education. The work of teachers is invariably rich in practical description, but rather sparse in 'explanation'.

In teaching personal and social education programmes at a comprehensive school in Dorset, Jean McNiff has explored the potential of action research as an approach to her professional development as she asked questions of the form, 'How do I improve this process of education here?'. She has produced a text to show what teachers have been able to achieve in starting their action enquiries with modest financial support from their authorities.

Jean argues that more case studies by academics of their own practice could lead to a transformation of the way we understand education – I agree. Yet my own work within the politics of educational knowledge would suggest that it is largely up to teachers to gain the initiative within the academic community by strengthening the explanatory power of their accounts of professional practice. I would go so far as to say that the development of our profession depends upon it. Teachers and local authority advisers should follow the lead provided by authorities such as Sheffield and ask for certification for teachers' descriptions and explanations of their own practice.

The strength of the action research approach to professional development rests upon a creative and critical dialogue between members of a community which includes teachers, academics, parents, students, industrialists and politicians. We move ahead through creative leaps of imagination. We learn from our mistakes in detailed criticisms of our positions. Jean McNiff is offering her work at a time of much strain, confusion and change. It is a timely invitation to help strengthen our profession through critical engagement in the concrete struggle to study practice from within. By focusing on the practical and theoretical questions of the kind, 'How do we improve the quality of education here?', I am confident that we will create improvements in the quality of education in a way which demonstrates the professional value of practical educational knowledge.

Whether we are successful could depend on your response to books such as this. Chapter 13 gives details of the work of individuals and networks whose development will depend upon your own practical commitment. Jean's purpose has been to produce a work which will enable you to identify with the difficulties, successes and failures which are part of an action enquiry. It portrays the ways in which teachers have started their enquiries. These beginnings can take a year or more. Those teachers who are fortunate to work in authorities such as Sheffield and Wiltshire where advisers have supported their enquiries over several years are beginning to produce case study research in sufficient numbers and of a quality which can demonstrate the large-scale potential of the approach to transform the world of educational practice and its theory. The evidence for the transformation is the improvement in the quality of education of ourselves and our students. While this book should be of use in getting your enquiry started it is likely that you will want to deepen your understanding of what is happening in your classroom in a way which will require timetabled release and in-service support from an institution of higher education. In this book Jean provides information on case studies which have benefited from this release and support. If you feel moved by this book to join us in our questioning of how to improve practice it will have served its purpose and made its contribution to the growth of a teacher-researcher movement committed to improving the quality of education with our students through our own professional development.

The book raises crucial questions for the providers of in-service education. There needs to be a much closer collaboration between the members of LEAs, institutions of higher education and schools – collaboration which should focus on the validation of teachers' claims to understand what they are doing with their pupils. It will only be through going public in this way that we will convince the community of the legitimacy of what we are doing. With this evidence we can embrace the accountability lobby with confidence.

Having briefly raised some implications which you may find in this book for yourself, your school, LEA and institution of higher education let me consider some international implications. If education is to lead us towards a more peaceful and productive world, we need a way of thinking about education which can be shared across national boundaries. My own study tours in Eastern Europe and the publications of the World Education Fellowship have convinced me of the use of action research as a way of understanding the values which are shared between educators across the world. We can start in a small way by examining the way our educational values are guiding our practice in our schools, colleges, polytechnics and universities. We should be prepared to see to what extent these values are universally shared, by subjecting them to the test of critical discussion within a democratic forum. It is this capacity of action research to hold together our individual practice with its universal significance which will, in my view, lead to improvements not only in our unique and personal contributions with our students but also to the education of our society and the world as a whole.

# Introduction

## The growing popularity of action research

Until the 1980s, probably the most frequent type of in-service support offered to practising teachers was in the form of taught courses. These courses were based either at a university or institute of higher education, or at an LEA or regional centre, or at a teachers' centre or other local/area centre. The courses usually focused on specific areas of concern in the curriculum, in order to improve the efficiency of schools and schooling.

There are two significant points here, and they will be recurring themes throughout. The first point is that of the control of educational knowledge, whether it is conveyed to teachers by others, or whether teachers are encouraged to find out for themselves. The second point is an implication, that of the aims of teaching. Teaching may be regarded as a means of improving schooling, by focusing on generalised issues of the management of curriculum or class, or it may be seen as a means of engaging in a critical process of action reflection which in itself is educational.

In the 1980s the emphasis has shifted from academy-based to teacher-centred educational research. The function of in-service education is changing from an improvement in schooling to an improvement in education. Action research is an alternative to the academy-based notion that, in order to qualify as a legitimate researcher, you need to be at a university, doing research on other people. The idea here is that a researcher is an expert. She passes on her theory, her version of the truth, to practising teachers in the classroom, and they put the theory into practice with their children. In research terms a teacher's performance is judged via educational theories drawn from the philosophy, psychology, sociology and history of education. Her performance is rarely judged in terms of criteria which look at the practical activity of education itself.

In the traditional form of in-service education, questions of education are approached from an 'objective' stance, where issues may be viewed by comparison with other issues. This approach is built on the notion of precedent; that the solution to a problem may be found by reference to the recorded solutions to other hypothetical problems. If I, as a teacher, am experiencing difficulties in my everyday class practice, I need to search the literature for projected answers. I look to the experts who have done all the work for me, put their ideas into practice, and I am regarded as a successful teacher by my headteacher, my colleagues, my adviser; but will my children benefit, and will I be satisfied in myself that I have found the most appropriate answer to my particular educational problem, here and now?

This approach to education, the view of a teacher as implementer of ideas, is a very popular view of educational research, and has been the overwhelmingly predominant theory as the basis of teacher competence (see, for example, Peters, 1966; Hirst, 1979; O'Connor, 1957). By sticking to this view, however, the assessors of educational efficiency are missing the most obvious point: that teachers are being encouraged, systematically and deliberately, to de-skill themselves. Instead of being encouraged to build up the wisdom to judge their own practice in terms of its educational competence, teachers are expected to implement identified criteria of excellence, to which they and their children are expected to conform. They are encouraged to 'come up to standard', but the standards are external to, and often have little bearing on, the reality of their immediate everyday practice. This view of teachers in classrooms denies them a self-image of reflective educators, and turns them simply into highly skilled technicians.

## Personal experience

I will illustrate these ideas by the reality of my own educational situation. For years I had been dissatisfied with my own class practice; the reality did not match my hopes. I taught mainly disadvantaged, disenchanted youngsters. I wanted to adopt an empathic style of teaching, but my children were unwilling to meet me. They were rude and aggressive, to each other and to me, and I found myself forced continually into an authoritarian role of keeping order and teaching by instruction. None of the books I read gave me enough specific guidance to solve the problem. Perhaps, I reasoned, I could find the answer if I tackled the problem as a research issue. I would go to the experts at university. Somewhere at the university, I felt sure, I would find the answers if I searched hard enough. Nobody told me, and I was not confident enough to realise that I had the answers all the time within my own professional practice and my own tacit knowledge.

I approached two different universities. Both welcomed me and my proposed project, and explained the strategies that we would adopt. 'Come to us,' said University A, 'and we will help you. We will first make available to you a taught course, so that you may study the disciplines of education. You will receive thorough training in the psychology, sociology and philosophy of education, and then you will be able to put these into practice by undertaking a research project for a term. After that you will receive your degree, and your thesis will take its rightful place on the university library shelves.' University B had different ideas. 'Come to us,' they said, 'and we will help you to rationalise the problem you are trying to solve. We will support you in your enquiry as you find its solution through your own practice. Your thesis will be the written version of your experience in working towards a solution, yours and the experiences of the other people involved in your project. Let us work together in a common endeavour to improve this particular process of education, both for yourself and the pupils in your care.'

Although at the time I was unaware of the principles in operation, the two interviews had made clear to me the differences between the conventional view of educational research, and the newer view of action research. I felt then simply that University A were giving me little freedom to explore my own interests; that they were taking my idea and re-shaping it to fit into their own framework. University B, I felt, would help me to follow through my problem (I was not even sure then what the problem was) and help me to find a practical solution. That was what I wanted and I enrolled there.

I feel that teachers are being misled by a view of controlled educational research. They are led to believe that, in order to qualify as a legitimate research proposal the field should not be of the 'ordinary' variety; that the researcher will have to set up an experimental situation and compare it with a 'normal' one; that she will have to quantify her findings; that all this will be conducted in an 'objective' fashion which will probably not make room for her own creativity; that in order to do her research, she will have to consult a university or other institution. Such a structured framework was indeed the view of the discredited 'disciplines' approach whose apparent inability to deal with such issues has given rise to the present crisis in educational theory. In this view educational research was split into its contributory disciplines of philosophy, psychology, sociology and history. Research in this tradition tended to be done on other people, rather than in a collaborative enquiry with them. Teachers' hopes of coming to grips with their everyday practical class problems were being deceived by the current insistence on this being the only acceptable view of research. Such an approach is clearly incapable of answering the commonplace, fundamentally crucial questions of 'How am I going to cope in tomorrow's lessons?', 'How am I going to improve the process of education for myself and my children?', 'Why am I failing?'.

There is a growing sense of frustration and dissatisfaction with this model at the grassroots level of the teaching profession. The disciplines approach to educational research became dominant in the 1960s and 1970s, but has begun to fall into decline in the 1980s. What is now needed is a coherent alternative, and an increasingly popular candidate appears to be action research.

This book attempts to put action research into perspective, socially, historically and educationally, with the hope that more and more teachers will be encouraged to regard themselves as legitimate investigators in their attempts to make sense of their own practice.

## Approaches to the theory of action research: a growing controversy

This could be, for some, a controversial text. My original intentions in writing it included the presentation of an overview of what was happening in action research, identifying key concepts in the movement, and attempting to show how one person's thinking may be moved forward by the contributions of others. As the correspondence has grown in the production of the text, however, it has become clear that there are quite different views about the philosophy of action research, and widely divergent opinions as to its application and contribution to educational thought.

University B on page xv was the University of Bath. There I met Jack Whitehead, the supervisor of my own PhD research project into personal and social education. I took action research as my preferred strategy of enquiry, and my reading in the field led me to believe that a great emphasis was placed on an approach to action research as a methodological issue, rather than a philosophical view of the nature of educational knowledge. This latter view is held by Jack, whose substantial writing tends to be published in the more academic journals and is largely inaccessible to busy working classroom teachers. I felt that the balance needed to be redressed.

The text has already received criticism from advocates of a more methodological approach. However, in producing the present text, my hope is that it will open up a debate that in itself will lead to increased insights as to the nature of the educational endeavour.

There does seem to be a polarisation between those working on action research in Cambridge and East Anglia, and at Bath. I do not present this text as a further weapon of divisiveness. I intend it to provide an accessible review and critique of the work going on in both centres. It would be well to remember in reading the book that some of the interpretations are my own, and that there is a focus towards the work that we are doing at Bath. I hope, however, that the focus does not distort the valuable work going on at other centres. My opinion is increasingly supported in the growing literature on action research that this approach is instrumental in taking the movement forward as an action-grounded philosophy of practitioner-centred research.

If my text is controversial, so be it. It will make its contribution by opening up a debate. In engaging in the debate, practitioners will of necessity assess, reason and give considered criticism of the issues; and in so doing will refine their insights as reflective practitioners.

## Audience

The book is intended for practising teachers, and for people who are actively involved in action research. It is intended to be used as an in-service resource. In-service education goes on in classrooms, teachers' centres and institutes of higher education; and the book is aimed at practising teachers in these locations. This means, of course, the teachers of the teachers as well, and it is hoped that the views presented in this book will be thought provoking and stimulating, providing a basis for the testing out of alternative theories within teachers' own practice.

Much of the literature to rationalise action research, that attempts to place it in an educational perspective, is difficult to read, often couched in language that is inaccessible to many people. I have endeavoured to present the ideas here in normal, easily comprehensible language, not intending to talk down to colleagues, but aware of the need for texts that get directly to the point.

At the same time I feel that, as a profession, we need to encourage the use of a common language for talking about educational practices. Staffrooms often deplore the use of technical terms, and keen teacher researchers are sometimes led to feel that they are above their station if they attempt to engage in conversations about the theory of education.

I plead for the adoption of in-service strategies that deliberately and systematically set out to encourage teachers to raise the level of their awarenesses. This means being open to new concepts, and developing an appropriate and efficient language as a currency for the exchange of those concepts. At the same time as attempting to make the language straightforward, I inevitably introduce terms and concepts that will at first seem unfamiliar. I have attempted to clarify them as the text progresses.

Teachers tend to be distrustful of educational research, seeing much of what goes on supposedly in their interests as largely irrelevant to the practical problems of today's lessons. Action research presents an opportunity for teachers to become uniquely involved in their own practice, to professionalise themselves, and to give reasoned justification for what they are doing. If this increased professionalism is to come about, teachers need to equip themselves with the practical and intellectual armoury to challenge established theories of education. This book aims to help this challenge and to contribute to the in-service revolution that is taking place.

## Structure of the book

The book is divided into three parts. Part I gives the background and explanations for action research. Part II shows the practicalities, giving the detail of actual research projects. Part III outlines some of the implications for teachers who embark on an action research project, the pitfalls as well as the satisfaction.

Each chapter is written as an independent unit that may be read in isolation without undue loss of continuity. Where appropriate, at the beginning of a chapter there is a brief synopsis of its content which will act as a quick guide to material which is expanded in the text.

As well as being a reference text, this book is intended to be an organic instrument in bringing people together.

I would be glad to hear from colleagues about aspects of their own research projects, with a view to improving the network that is already functioning.

*Jean McNiff*
1988

# PART I

# BACKGROUND AND EXPLANATIONS

# Chapter 1

# What Action Research is: Its Uses and Limitations

## Introduction

Action research is the name given to an increasingly popular movement in educational research. It encourages a teacher to be reflective of his own practice in order to enhance the quality of education for himself and his pupils. It is a form of self-reflective enquiry that is now being used in school-based curriculum development, professional development, school-improvement schemes, and so on, and, as such, it actively involves teachers as participants in their own educational process.

The movement is growing in credibility and is now seen in educational communities as a real alternative to the more traditional theory-based approach to educational research. This approach reduces educational theory and research to the separate disciplines of the sociology, psychology, history and philosophy of education. Action research approaches education as a unified exercise, seeing a teacher in class as the best judge of his total educational experience. It is a powerful method of bridging the gap between the theory and practice of education; for here teachers are encouraged to develop their own personal theories of education from their own class practice.

## Characterisations of action research

The literature of action research is growing rapidly. As it grows, so do the number of definitions and characterisations. Educational action research may be seen variously as an umbrella term for what goes on in class when a teacher decides to change a taken-for-granted situation and opts to become the researcher of his own class practice (for example, Hustler *et al.*, 1986); or it may be viewed as a recipe or blueprint for teacher action (for example, Elliott, 1981).

The first perspective describes the outcomes when a teacher decides to intervene in his own practice. The literature offers various definitions for this intervention such as 'classroom research' (Hopkins, 1985), 'self-reflective enquiry' (Kemmis, 1982), and 'action research' (Hustler *et al.*, 1986). In this sense, there is no hard and fast definition of what happens. Action research is seen as a way of characterising a loose set of activities that are designed to improve the quality of education; it is an essentially eclectic way in to a self-reflective programme aimed at such educational improvement. The second perspective attempts to identify the criteria of these activities; to formulate systems that will account for the improvement that is an anticipated outcome of the self-reflective programme. In this sense, the term action research is a term used to describe methods and techniques.

There are a number of definitions available in the literature (see, for instance, Rapoport, 1970; Elliott, 1981; Ebbutt, 1983). Perhaps the most widely accepted working definition is that provided by Stephen Kemmis of Deakin University, together with Wilf Carr of the University College of North Wales:

> Action research is a form of self-reflective enquiry undertaken by participants (teachers, students or principals, for example) in social (including educational) situations in order to improve the rationality and justice of (a) their own social or educational practices, (b) their understanding of these practices, and (c) the situations (and institutions) in which these practices are carried out.
>
> (Carr and Kemmis, 1986)

As with any emergent movement, interpretations will vary and probably increase. The main focus of action research in classrooms and schools, however, is to encourage teachers to become involved in their own practice, and to view themselves as researchers (Stenhouse, 1975). Walker (1985) makes this point in the last sentence of his book, when he says: 'In that sense, the book begins here, at the point when the reader becomes the active researcher'. That is exactly the point of this present book: to clarify issues; to present some signposts; and to encourage teachers to become researchers in their own classrooms.

## Rationale for action research

The social basis of action research is involvement; the educational basis is improvement. Its operations demand changes. Action research means ACTION, both of the system under consideration, and of the people involved in that system. System can mean any human social order – factories, airlines, services, schools – and people means all personnel, not just the managers, for in a democratic system the smallest part will affect the overall shape of the whole. Within a system, one aspect of it might be identified as a problem area; so, for example, a teacher could focus on one limited part of his class practice. On the other hand he could find that his actions in solving the problem will have repercussions for wider aspects of the school society and its personnel. For example, John M., concerned that he was having discipline problems in one class, found that he was aggravating the situation by going on at his pupils about their poor behaviour. He discovered that, if he adopted an alternative style, the problems disappeared. His amended style involved a negotiation, an establishment of ground rules for conduct in class, which everyone agreed and abided by. He was then encouraged to explore the possibilities and refinements of such a style in his other classes, and to enlist the participation of other colleagues. Some colleagues in turn saw the benefits of his new style, and decided to try it out for themselves. The group of teachers exchanged ideas continually, learning from each other in an environment of public support for their systematic enquiry.

As a method of exploring and solving problem issues, action research can be applied equally to large-scale enquiries. Kurt Lewin, the man who popularised the name, was himself involved in improving relations in industrial situations. He saw this sort of participatory procedure as much more effective in solving problems of human interrelationships than an imposed, structured process, into which people were expected to fit. Square pegs tend to resent being forced into round holes. Lewin saw this idea of involvement and participation as a way of accommodating the square pegs, or, perhaps, changing the shape of the round holes. Accommodation and change are all part of the democratic process which allows for individual differences and creative episodes; indeed, individualities will themselves shape the environment. The action of action research, whether on a small or large scale, implies change in people's lives, and therefore in the system in which they live.

This point highlights one of the questions to do with educational research in general: action research attempts to answer the 'macro-micro' problem. This is the point that, depending on the outlook of the researcher, the study can be pitched at different levels of social and educational complexity. Education may be viewed as a total social concept which acts as a cultural framework for the individual, or it may be seen from a 'client-centre', as being to do with the development of individuals in society. The methods of action research are equally applicable to large-scale as well as small-scale enquiries, taking the view that the individual may give explanations for his own professional and personal development; and in turn his considered actions will contribute to the shaping of a future society. This question is dealt with more fully in Chapter 10.

Applied to classrooms, action research is an approach to improving education through change, by encouraging teachers to be aware of their own practice, to be critical of that practice, and to be prepared to change it. It is participatory, in that it involves the teacher in his own enquiry, and collaborative, in that it involves other people as part of a shared enquiry. It is research WITH, rather than research ON.

This point is very important. Popular notions of educational research are often distortions and myths. The prevailing idea of the traditional approach is that the researcher, the expert, does all the research on other people. Teachers are often wary of such self-appointed experts who use schools, pupils and teachers as data-fodder to provide the results they have 'decided on in advance'. The supposition is that the expert has a hypothesis he wants to test – or has a fairly clear idea as to his objectives – and he conducts experiments on other people to corroborate his hypothesis. This approach is dangerous when the enquiry is to do with humans. It is all very well if the subject matter is to do with objectively verifiable issues. It is foolish, however, to speak of control groups when those groups are made up of people. Although there are many areas of human behaviour that are predictable in varying degrees – many of these behaviours in pedagogic settings – fundamental criteria of humanity are its creativity and unpredictability. People are as likely to be surprised by their own behaviour as an external researcher.

For example, suppose that a teacher wanted to find out if a different approach to talking time in class would affect pupil performance. If he encouraged the children to ask questions freely, or to work in pairs or groups, rather than primarily to listen to his explanations or read books, would their understanding of the subject matter be enhanced?

A traditional view of research would suggest setting up such an experimental group and measuring their progress by means of tests. The results of these tests would be matched against those of children who were part of a control group. According to the results of the tests, the teacher would have passed or failed in his new methodology. It is of concern that many teachers find they cannot squeeze themselves into an imposed structure of educational research, and then feel that they have failed because there is a misfit. Action research takes the view that it is not the fit that is at fault, but the whole concept that people will obligingly fall into categories and systems and react in accordance with the theory of working parts.

This machine-mindedness is the basis of the traditional view of educational research. It is based on a method which tries to measure and quantify, as if people are entirely predictable. Action research attempts to make sense of situations from a completely different stand. If this method views its functions as problem solving, then action research may be seen as problem posing. It is a search for the right questions appropriate to educational situations as well as their answers.

In the example, the teacher would want to ask questions about his practice. Why was he dissatisfied with the present situation? What was he going to change? How would he observe the reactions? How would he evaluate those reactions? And how would he change his practice to accommodate his findings? It is the questions of educational research that are important, the questions that a teacher is prepared to ask himself about what is going on in his class, and his preparation to answer them honestly and with due regard to the possible consequences. Those consequences will almost certainly imply a change, but it is a change that is going to lead to an improvement. That improvement would not have come about if he had not in the first place been aware or sensitive to his own professional standards. Action research is an instrument used wilfully by good teachers to improve their practice.

Yet one of the challenges to action research is that it is what good teachers are supposed to be doing anyway; that is, being continually aware of their class practice and attempting to improve that practice. This, say the sceptics, is not research but just good teaching. Action research goes further than this, and is itself a vehicle for enhancing the teaching–learning situation. Action research is not just teaching. It is being aware and critical of that teaching, and using this self-critical awareness to be open to a process of change and improvement of practice. It encourages teachers to become adventurous and critical in their thinking, to develop theories and rationales for their practice, and to give reasoned justification for their public claims to professional knowledge. It is this systematic ENQUIRY MADE PUBLIC which distinguishes the activity as research.

For example, Janet M. is involved in introducing schemes of personal and social education into her school. This is a value-saturated area of the curriculum, and any enhancement in the children's behaviour and attitudes defies quantification. 'How,' asks Janet, 'can you "measure" whether the children have become more sensitive, or more aware, or more tolerant? How can you measure being nice?' She began her enquiry within a disciplines framework, and the advice she was given by her adviser was to administer pre-attitude tests, teach 'the course', and then administer post-attitude tests. The statistical data she received from the tests would indicate the amount of 'progress' the pupils had 'achieved'. This strategy was quite inapplicable to Janet's needs, and alien to her concept of what personal and social education was all about. For her, personal and social education is a total educational concept, involving all aspects of the curriculum, and not just 'the course'. The 'progress' of the children could not be viewed as a linear progression of (1) surly, (2) acceptable, (3) polite, but involved their self-commitment as a way of life, an in-dwelling rather than a putting on and taking off. Yet, if Janet was not going to quote statistical evidence that the children had gained from her, how was she to justify her claim to her own educational knowledge, that the children and she had benefited as persons through their work and life together? How was she to respond to her colleagues who would claim, 'But these improvements in the children may well have happened without you.'?

Action research resolves to give reasoned justification to claims to professional knowledge. Janet could say in response to the challenging questions: 'True, but if you will consider my practice, I hope to demonstrate actively that they ARE happening WITH me. I can show you documentary evidence that will indicate how I found my practice unsatisfactory, how I thought about it and changed it as necessary, in discussion with others. Then I can show you evidence on video and audiotape, where the children say that they have changed because of our joint involvement. And then you, as colleagues, can agree or disagree with me that they have moved from where they were, as seen on the video of last December, to where they are now, in June; and we can identify together criteria that we will agree indicate that movement.' It is this conjoint experiencing, this mutually supportive dialogue, that is the action of research that brings people together as explorers of their own destiny, rather than alienates them as operators and puppets.

Action research is systematic. It is, as Lawrence Stenhouse requires (1980), 'a systematic enquiry made public'. It is not the random, *ad hoc* activity that characterises everyday life, although it accommodates within its method those random, surprise elements of unpredictability and creation. The method itself of action research is elegant. It involves a self-reflective spiral of planning, acting, observing, reflecting and re-planning. It requires teachers to be acutely aware of a sense of process, and to refine their perceptions to account for that process. Far from being *ad hoc* and woolly, action research raises to a conscious level much of what is already being done by good teachers on an intuitive level. It enables teachers to identify and come to grips with their practice in a humane way which is at once supportive and critical. As a headmaster said of his staff: 'It liberates teachers from their prejudices and allows their instincts to blossom.'

## Uses and limitations

At the same time, action research is not the only answer to any and every educational problem. There are some areas of concern where an alternative approach may be more appropriate, such as issues based on statistical analyses or comparative studies, where human unpredictability is not the issue, or where a straightforward comparison between introductory and control situations is required. For interpersonal issues – for example, establishing helping relationships, different teaching styles, assessment of the appeal of texts – action research is a very useful strategy. It can take a broadly based liberal approach to such issues. It can conduct its enquiry in a human fashion, taking one-to-one relationships between persons as its centre of gravity. For enquiries that rest on a hard-nosed analysis of data, however, action research is inappropriate. For that, statistical methodologies are necessary.

It has been said (for example, Reason and Rowan, 1981) that this 'new paradigm research' is softer, more feminine in its approach. 'A new regime of softness' appears on the cover of their book. The validity of the approach lies in the skills of the enquirer; it is more personal and interpersonal, rather than methodological (p. 244). This does not imply that the activities and formulations of action research are sloppy or ill planned. It means rather that action research has as its philosophical base an overarching awareness and respect for the integrity of individuals, a quality that is often lacking in the more traditional theory-based approaches to educational research. Yet, while it is evident that action research is not always an answer to the solving of educational dilemmas, its humanistic basis can make a contribution to the use of statistics-based and other theories in the empiric tradition (see page 11).

It is worth making two points here. First, a theory has no real value unless it can be demonstrated to have practical implications. The work of Schutz (1972), Gadamer (1975) and Habermas (1979) takes this point as fundamental. It is in the living reality of people that thought is turned into action.

So, while an empirical theory (such as a statistics-based approach) to an educational issue may be the most useful, the theory that is generated must be tested in practice, its data must be collated and analysed, and action must be taken on the analysis. All these steps are performed by people, either on a distanced basis as in programming the computer that will do the mechanics, or on a particularly personal basis, as in discussing the analysis and its applications. Another slogan that appears in Reason and Rowan (1981) is 'research can never be neutral'. Indeed, the applications of empiric theories are far from neutral; it is people who make the decisions about selections and applications, and people whose lives are affected by those decisions. The educational research that leads to educational theory is by its nature implicational; it cannot be seen in a people-free vacuum, otherwise it has no reason.

The second point is that action research is an approach to solving educational problems that has evolved out of previous theories. It does not now reject those theories as being wrong. It shifts the emphasis and perspective. Kuhn (1962) points out that the emergence of a new approach is often accompanied by a sense of crisis in the established paradigm. Theories are not born and killed, but may be gradually synthesised into new patterns. The elegance of action research is that it possesses within itself the ability to incorporate previous approaches, simply because its focus rests on the enquirer rather than his methodology. It is primarily his insights and understandings that are moved forward by his own involvement in his enquiry.

To summarise, although it is fair to say that other approaches may be appropriate for certain educational issues, the principles of action research may be used by the researcher to move forward his own conduct in the enquiry. By adopting a humanistic view of the nature of educational enquiry he turns his endeavour into a human enquiry. He equips himself more rationally to select his philosophical base and his methodology, and to apply wisdom in the analysis of the data. Most importantly, he accepts as a tenet that any proposed application of the analyses affects the lives of real people. In this way, research becomes political. Action research highlights the need for democratic participation, no matter what the preferred theory or strategy, in the implicational phase of educational research.

## Conclusion

Action research implies adopting a deliberate openness to new experiences and processes, and, as such, demands that the action of educational research is itself educational. By consciously engaging in their own educational development, teachers gain both professionally and personally; and it is this personal commitment that counts in the process of human enquiry. Without personal commitment, teaching is no more than what appears on the curriculum, and learning the product of a schooled society. For if we as teachers are truly to fulfil our obligations as educators, then we must accept the responsibility of first educating ourselves.

# Chapter 2

# Action Research as an Educational Tradition

## Introduction

There are certain assumptions about educational research which shape educationists' thinking and determine policy. This chapter looks at some of those traditions and attempts to put action research into historical, social and educational perspective. It also gives a rationale why action research is probably more useful to the needs of teachers in the living systems of their own classrooms than theories that are often more sociological than educational.

Educational research may be approached from different perspectives, depending on the aims of the research and the constraints on the researcher. In Britain there are two broad categories of established research traditions: the empiricist and the interpretive (Adelman and Young, 1985). In this chapter it is suggested that action research offers the new perspective of an educational tradition.

Inevitably, when discussing the emergence of new ideas, there is some notion of history involved. There is not scope in this book to go into a detailed chronological history of the educational movements that have encouraged the evolution of action research. An excellent account is offered in Carr and Kemmis *Becoming Critical* (1986). What is suggested in this chapter is that action research gives a new dimension to educational research, a dimension that enables it to live up to its title of educational.

In his essay, 'Why educational research has been so uneducational: a case for a new model of social science based on collaborative inquiry' (1981), William Torbert investigates the gap between educational theory and educational practice. 'Why hasn't past educational research taught us better educational practice?' he asks, and suggests as an answer that 'the reasons why neither current practice nor current research helps us to identify and move towards good educational practice is that both are based on a model of reality that emphasises unilateral control for gaining information from, or having effects on, others.'

It is suggested in this book that a research tradition that encourages teachers to investigate their own practice on the job will by definition be educational, in that it attempts to make sense of the reality of immediate situations and enables enquirers to account for their own educational development. They can say why they felt dissatisfied with previous practice, and how they set about changing it. They can present some form of evidence to show their improved present practice, and they are able to describe the intervening action that has led to this situation. It is this ability to explain the process and present evidence to back up their claims of improvement that is inherent in the notion of teachers' educational development.

## The empiricist tradition

At the heart of this tradition is the idea of evidence being empirically tested: that is, the only valid data is what is directly experienced through the senses. Knowledge of educational practice is collected in terms of what can be observed. It is an assumption that data is gathered about other people's practice by an external recorder, and it is his interpretation of that practice that provides the substance of the research. Research is about other people, seeking to observe, record and analyse, what Pike (1967) has called the etic approach. The actor in the research – the teacher in class, for example – is not consulted about the methods, the aims or the reasons for the research. The researcher is regarded as a reliable interpreter of the action, since he is external to it and can therefore make objective comments about what is going on. Interference by the actor is regarded as contaminating, in that his personal opinion might skew otherwise objectively determinable facts.

The empiricist tradition has an application in many spheres, including some pedagogic settings (see page 75), where the emphasis is on data collection and its statistical analysis, and where the issue is not one of personal development. Market surveys, for example, rely on this approach, with extended use of questionnaires and interviews.

The data gathered will throw light on the researcher's questions: 'Which is the most popular brand of the product?' for example. 'How many people read a certain newspaper?' In pedagogic settings, such an approach will help in questions such as: 'How many children reached a certain level of achievement in the test? Have attendance figures improved over the last three years?' Questions which attempt to answer subjects', including teachers', problems regarding practice and its effects on the clients are not usually formulated in this tradition. A question of the type 'How can *I* explain and improve this situation?' are not accommodated.

Embedded in this tradition is the idea of positivism. This term applies to research methods that are used in analysing and explaining natural phenomena, such as judging whether a certain type of vegetable is better through the use of additives, or if polystyrene packaging is safer than other materials. The ways in which these judgements are reached are standardised and try to eliminate human error. They include using control groups, statistical analysis of data, pre- and post-testing. This 'scientific method' maintains that results may be predicted and environments may be controlled to ensure that those results really do come about. So if the aim is to produce a superior quality of vegetable through the use of certain additives, control groups of vegetables will be compared with experimental groups, the results compared, and the research findings put into wider application if the results warrant it. There is a distinct cause and effect relationship here.

When this view is applied to educational research, it aims to produce a theory that sees educational phenomena as parallel to natural phenomena, and the same methods are used to evaluate them. All things are seen as predictable, regular, and capable of being fitted into the pre-determined structure.

Much educational research over the past thirty years has followed the empiricist positivist line. Behavioural psychology, for example, is based on the notion of cause and effect. If I arrange appropriate stimuli (Skinner, 1968), I can expect certain accelerated responses; if I arrange the conditions of learning (Gagné, 1965) in a certain way, then my pupils will be more inclined to learn what I want them to learn; if I determine in advance the objectives I want to achieve (Mager, 1962), then my practice will aim to bring about these objectives.

## Critique of the empiricist tradition

There are very important implications in this view of controlled, empirical knowledge. Three of the most important in terms of educational theory are its management, its epistemology (the knowledge base) and its social organisation.

The management of an educational research situation, following the empiricist tradition, is geared towards answering the questions of the external researcher, rather than those of the teacher. The two sets of questions may sometimes be far apart, with the researcher asking questions of the sort, 'How many children reach a certain level of achievement in, say, a reading test?', and the teacher asking, 'Why has such a low percentage of the children "succeeded" and what can I do to improve the achievement levels of the others?' The researcher's questions stress his need to know certain data, and his analysis of the data will probably be used in substantiating his own hypothesis about this educational setting. This setting is often viewed as a sample, a 'one of many', that may be compared with others; the data, its analysis and subsequent applications will be regarded in the same way as that of other educational situations. Following this approach, one classroom is much the same as another, and questions of teaching and learning may be solved by a recipe that will be suggested by the researcher. There is little attention paid to the personal theories of teachers, that take as their epistemological base questions of the type, 'How can I improve this process of education here?' (Whitehead, 1977). 'Why is my present practice unsatisfactory? How can I develop my own personal and professional expertise to deal with the problem, and give reasoned justification for my actions?'

The epistemology of the empiricist tradition is that theory determines practice. Teachers are encouraged to fit their practice into a stated theory, and this can often lead to malaise. The approach itself and the theory it generates are often couched in terms of the control of teachers' practice. Aspects of our educational system, based on this view of research, may be seen as linear, with overtones of line-management. In this tradition, the view of education is that it is basically a commodity, with certain bits more or less useful than others. Teachers are not encouraged to decide for themselves what is most useful and appropriate, but perform according to the theory. This approach tends to encourage stasis rather than development.

For example, Brian Green (1979) wanted to improve his understanding of his art education. He tells how he originally tried to use the traditional techniques of questionnaires and observation schedules. 'I focused my work on trying to understand the interactions between the teacher and pupils by using a psychological observation schedule,' he records. 'This was an approach . . . to try and explain the process of education in an art lesson. I ultimately rejected this approach.' He did so because (1) the categories given did not reflect the reality of his classroom, (2) 'arriving at an idea of "style" was not very helpful in explaining the process of education', and (3) the categories were inappropriate for his particular situation. This teacher's experience echoes that of many other teachers who feel that they have to turn their own natural practice into an artificial exercise in order to meet the theory that they are supposed to use in order to explain that practice. It is difficult to break out of this tradition if it is seen as the accepted and correct way, and if no viable alternatives are presented (see Chapter 12).

The social organisation of an empirical approach to educational research has serious implications for the concept of teachers as autonomous educators. The theory that results implies control; it does not encourage teachers to be adventurous and creative in their practice, nor to be personally reflective and critical of that practice. This approach accords little value to the concept of teachers as educators. The business of being an educator carries a heavy moral charge, and for teachers to be entrusted with this charge, they must be credited with their appropriate status as philosophers and practitioners. As it is, the empiricist tradition at best views teachers as technicians. This is a massive point to ponder for those who would be assessors of teachers' performance; for is our in-service provision aiming to turn out technicians or educators? And in what terms are they to be judged? For if teachers are judged in the light of an epistemology that has a notion of controlled educational knowledge as its basis, then all we are looking for is slick operators; but if we are truly looking for educators, then an alternative approach to educational theory must be embraced.

## The interpretive tradition

The empiricist approach insists on an 'objective' recording and interpretation of data, with any intervention by the actor-researchee as possibly contaminating the results. The interpretive approach acknowledges that the actor's accounts are as valid as those of the observer. It is important in this approach that the actors and the observers agree their interpretations, and disagreements between them often provide a rich field for the research study, in trying to decide where the mismatch lies and to resolve it.

This tradition is essentially sociological. It has its roots in the work of American sociologists in the early twentieth century. Its ascendancy can be seen in the work of Glaser and Strauss (1964), who constantly compare instances of practice as examples of the total body of practice; and Parlett and Hamilton (1972) who developed the idea of 'progressive focusing', which is identifying key points within the data and continually homing in on the central issues.

There is a clear debt in this tradition to anthropology and ethnography, fields which focus on the integrity of people, individually and in social groups. Notably Levi-Strauss (for example, 1968) insists on the actors' accounts only as being valid interpretations of the data – an emic approach as opposed to etic, that is personal accounts and understandings as opposed to observers'. The interpretive tradition focuses on comparing and attempting to resolve the discrepancies between the etic and the emic, the observers and the actors.

During the 1960s and 1970s a type of ethnographic research developed which was characterised in several ways. One term that made a lasting impact was that of 'illuminative evaluation' (Parlett and Hamilton, 1972) but it was gradually re-cast as 'case study'. The advocates of a case-study approach point out that it is naturalistic, involving the people who would naturally be participants in the research, for example teachers, and democratic, in that the actors' opinions are as valid as the observers' (see, for example, Walker, 1982).

The methods of the empiricist tradition operate mainly from a statistical, quantitative base; the interpretive tradition looks more at qualitative analysis of data. Case study appeals to the 'grounded theory' of Glaser and Strauss (1967) in that the knowledge and interpretation of educational phenomena must be grounded in the reality of class practice. It employs skills appropriate to sociological research such as triangulation. Elliott and Adelman (1976) explain that

> Triangulation involves gathering accounts of a teaching situation from three quite different points of view; namely, those of the

> teacher, his pupils, and a participant observer. Who in the 'triangle' gathers the accounts, how they are elicited, and who compares them, depends largely on the context. . . . By comparing his own account with accounts from the other two standpoints a person as one point of the triangle has an opportunity to test and perhaps revise it on the basis of more sufficient data.

*The disciplines approach*

As a spin-off from educational theories cast in the empiricist and interpretive traditions, a 'disciplines' approach emerged. This was a body of general educational theory which was more concerned with the initial training of teachers and with matters of curriculum than with how educational research should be carried out.

This approach divided educational theory into the different disciplines of philosophy, sociology, history and psychology. It began in the work of Louis Arnaud Reid, the first Professor of Philosophy at the London Institute.

In the 1960s there was an emphasis on synthesising the separate disciplines to provide a common focus. This movement was mainly associated with the writings of Professors Richard Peters and Paul Hirst of the London Institute. Peters maintains:

> . . . the different disciplines must mesh in with each other in relation to matters of educational policy and practice . . .
>
> (Peters, 1977)

while Hirst says:

> Educational principles are justified entirely by direct appeal to knowledge from a variety of forms, scientific, philosophical, historical, etc. Beyond these forms of knowledge it requires no theoretical synthesis.
>
> (Hirst, 1966, p. 55)

The long history of controlled knowledge found vigorous supporters in Peters and Hirst. In their 1970 *Logic and education* (p. 15) they maintain:

> It is the purpose of this book to show the ways in which such a view of education must impose such a structure on our practical decisions . . . and . . . impose its stamp on the curriculum.
>
> (Hirst and Peters, 1970)

Their views were very powerful, and have provided the basis for much educational thought for the last twenty years. Psychology and sociology particularly have been seen as crucial sources of educational knowledge and have dominated much 'educational' research. Their approach was much weakened in 1983 (see below), yet, even though it attempted to bring the fragmented disciplines together by a coherent theory, that theory still took as its ideological basis the stamp of authority.

## Critique of the interpretive tradition

There are three main areas of concern in using this approach in an educational study.

The first point is the inherent weakness in case study as a legitimate research design. Case study is often accused of being woolly with little scientific rigour. Hamilton (1980) denies this vigorously. Yet many critics claim that it lacks rigour and a recognisable methodology (see, for example, Atkinson and Delamont, 1985).

A further criticism of case study is that the 'case' itself is often ill-defined, and the term is in danger of losing credibility. Case study is often described as 'the study of an instance in action' or 'bounded system', but, as Stake points out:

> The case need not be a person or enterprise. It can be whatever 'bounded system' (to use Louis Smith's term) that is of interest. An institution, a program, a responsibility, a collection, or a population can be the case.
>
> (Stake, 1980)

The vagueness and confusion that this statement suggests weakens the academic legitimacy of case study as a rigorously scientific research method.

The second point is the ascendancy of the notion of the disciplines of educational knowledge, and the adoption of a research strategy that perpetuates the divisions. Psychology and sociology have been viewed particularly as crucial sources. The concept of education, however, is more than the sum of its parts. Hirst acknowledged this in 1983, saying that he had been mistaken in his thinking, and viewed educational theory now as having to be tested against the reality of practice in order to be valid. By adopting this stand, Hirst contributed much to the restructuring of the image of educational research, as being of direct use to teachers in attempting to make sense of their own practice. From a traditionally 'disciplines' focus, educational research is being increasingly seen as having an immediately practical use as an in-service resource.

A third and consequent criticism of case study and the interpretive tradition as a whole is that the methods of interpretive enquiry are more appropriate to sociological issues than educational; and that the notion of educational knowledge is seen as a controlled commodity. The methods of data collection, analysis and synthesis are different from those of the empiricist tradition, one emphasising the quantitative and the other the qualitative; but the concept of control by the researcher of the researchee is equally apparent in both. Consider, for example, that the questions asked of the research proposal would be much the same in the interpretive tradition as in the empiricist: 'Why do we need to look at this instance here?' 'What results do we hope to achieve from our research intervention?' 'What is in it for us?' 'Can we compare this case with any precedent?' 'Can we all finally agree an original hypothesis?' Supporters of an interpretive approach would insist that it was democratic and humanitarian, but it is evident from the whole design that the researcher is still imposing a framework into which the researchee must fit himself and his practice. The request of the interpretive researcher is: 'Let me look at what you are doing here. I think I know what you are doing; but I will listen to what you think you are doing, and together we will work towards a true account of your practice.' Such an approach is not by itself educational, in that it does not encourage a teacher to review his own practice, to make suggestions as to how to move forward that practice and his understanding of his own educational development.

Both the empiricist and the interpretive traditions are grounded in subjects other than educational practice. They do not allow for such questions as 'How can I improve my class practice?' or 'How can I account for my own educational development?' – first, because it is not part of their methodological design to ask such practical, problem-based questions, and second, because it is not part of their conceptual repertoire to answer them. They can make predictions and give descriptions of the phenomena of social settings. They cannot give educational explanations for the events within those settings. For that, another sort of approach is needed, one that will tackle the practical issues of why things happen as they do, rather than as they might.

What is needed is a new educational tradition, a coherent approach to the everyday practice and problems of teachers in ordinary classrooms who are trying to understand and make sense of their professional and personal lives.

## The educational tradition

In 1953, Stephen Corey's book, *Action research to improve school practices*, was published. This was the first systematic attempt to define action research in education. Corey says that the expression 'action research' and the operations it implies come from at least two independent sources. The first source was from Collier, Commissioner for Indian Affairs from 1933–45. He used the expression to plea for a joint approach by layman and administrator to research. The second source was Kurt Lewin, working in America and keen to study human relationships scientifically and to encourage people to improve their relationships through their own enquiries. Lewin (1946) formulated a schema to enable people to conduct their own systematic enquiries. This schema was very influential and provided the basis for the refinements of Kemmis, Elliott and Ebbutt (see Chapter 3).

After the first initial enthusiasm generated by Corey's book, the idea of action research lost momentum. Educational action research was replaced by the Research, Development and Diffusion model (see page 24). This was a model favoured in the 1960s, in America and in Britain, centrally funded, and undertaken on a large scale as opposed to individualised, small-scale action research projects. These approaches have lost credibility in the 1970s and 1980s because of the shrinkage of central funds, and the dissatisfaction with the RD and D model, basically a top-down approach.

In America, the impetus for the new concept of teacher as researcher came from an influential paper by J. J. Schwab, 'The practical: a language for the curriculum' (1969). The mood in America was inward-turning. There was unease and protest against pressure on the individual. The Korean war, McCarthyism, the Vietnam war, increasing insistence on technological control of systems, all made their mark. The scene was set for action research as a localised methodology that made the individual the centrepiece of educational theory.

In Britain in the 1960s and 1970s similar moves were afoot in the work of Lawrence Stenhouse and the Humanities Curriculum Project. He took as his central thesis the idea of teacher as researcher. He saw development and research as closely related, and required practising teachers to reflect critically and systematically about their practice. For him, the teacher was a central agent in the research process and as such had to empower himself as a professional. This required the development of a clear sense of resolve, a dedication to acquiring practical skills, and a committed desire to scrutinise personal practice.

Stenhouse was based at the Centre of Applied Research in Education (CARE) at the University of East Anglia, as were his colleagues and collaborators, John Elliott and Clem Adelman, joint directors of the Ford Teaching Project. This project also focused on curriculum research and development through the eyes of practising teachers.

At the same time (1976), at the University of Bath, Jack Whitehead was working with groups of teachers as part of the Schools Council Mixed Ability Exercise in Science. He was deeply concerned that teachers should receive support in their enquiries about their own educational practices. His aim was – and still is – to set up networks of support for teachers in classrooms to regard themselves as legitimate researchers.

As time has gone on, the two groups have developed along different lines (see Chapter 3) in terms of the applications of action research, but they remain constant in their view of its function. Here is a possible answer to the deficiencies of research traditions that have been sociology, rather than education, based. Carr and Kemmis (1986) coined the phrase 'educational action research'. From its sociological base with Lewin, it has been applied directly to the field of education, not only to observe, record and describe the work in that field, but to widen the perspective and make the investigation itself educational. Anyone who becomes involved in the enquiry is committed, and it is this act of commitment to improvement and to reflect on consequences that is educational.

It is evident from this very brief survey that action research can offer a devolution of power from the universities to the classroom, from the external researcher to the teacher as researcher. In the next chapter I shall attempt to show the thinking behind this devolution and the emergence of the need for strategic action research.

# Chapter 3

# Some Current Trends in Action Research Thinking

## Introduction

Practices are the nub of action research. This chapter gives an account of some of the key concepts that have emerged to date, to show how they attempt to give a practice-centred rationale for their theories. Some thinkers have given a theoretical form to action research, that is, come up with a formal organisation for devising solutions for the everyday difficulties of classroom life. It would be unwise to say that these theories resulted in models. The word 'model' suggests a prescriptive element that may encourage teachers to regard what they read as a final state of the art. This smacks of positivism. Action research is never static. The term itself implies a continual process, a search. It is a process which shows how one person's ideas develop and may be used by another to move his own ideas forward.

It must be stressed that the views presented in this chapter are my own. Although I offer criticism of some of the work to date, I have tried to present that work fairly and as representative of its creator.

The chapter is in five sections:

1 The seminal work of Kurt Lewin
2 Lawrence Stenhouse: his work and influence
3 The formal schemes of Stephen Kemmis, John Elliott and Dave Ebbutt
4 Jack Whitehead and his notion of a living educational theory
5 Advancing the theory: an individual teacher as a maker of theory grounded in practice

There are of course many eminent thinkers who have moved forward the ideas of action research through their work and publications. Their omission in this chapter is not to deny the value of their work, nor the debt of gratitude owed to them by those persons who do appear in this chapter.

## 1 The seminal work of Kurt Lewin

Kurt Lewin, a social psychologist, was keen to study social issues himself, and also to provide people with an instrument to study their own relationships. He felt that the best way to move people forward was to engage them in their own enquiries into their own lives. As the basis of his ideas he stressed the importance of democratic collaboration and participation. It is no use people enquiring on their own, for they are part of the life of other people. It is no use standing to one side, for we are all parties in the human endeavour.

Lewin described action research as a spiral of steps. Each step had four stages: planning, acting, observing, reflecting. (*Note*: the following examples and those on pp. 27 and 28 and the following diagrams are the author's.)

The scheme in action looks like this:

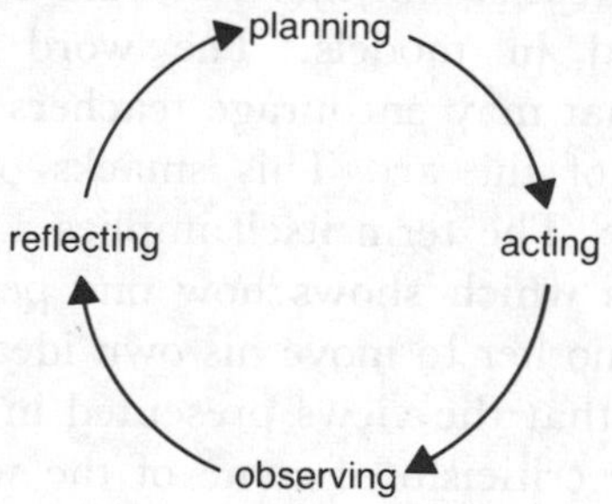


*Fig. 3.1*

*Example 1*

*Planning*: How can I make my dog better behaved? Perhaps I should take him to training classes.

*Acting*: I take him to training classes.

*Observing*: I see how the dogs behave at class.

*Reflecting*: Perhaps I should do the same at home in a consistent fashion.

*Example 2*

*Planning*: I need to make communication in the office more effective. I shall issue weekly information sheets to the staff.

*Acting*: I issue the sheets.

*Observing*: Conversations with the staff indicate that they are more aware of overall issues.

*Reflecting*: But I do not know what they think. How do I get efficient feedback?

This step would then move on to the next step of re-planning, acting, observing, reflecting, and perhaps produce a whole series of steps:

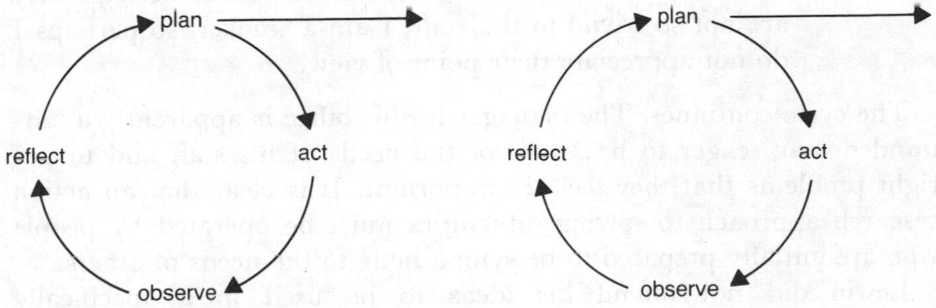


*Fig. 3.2*

Example 2 can then be extended:

*Planning*: Perhaps I should set up some sort of open communication channel.

*Acting*: I install a suggestions box.

*Observing*: The suggestions in the box suggest that (1) I appoint a liaison officer, (2) I hold weekly (democratic) staff meetings.

*Reflecting*: This is not a bad idea. I must be careful not to lose overall control, though. How shall I set about becoming democratic?

*Planning*: I shall invite Mrs Jones to be an informal liaison officer on a pro tem basis.
I shall publish an agenda for a staff meeting and invite staff to submit items for inclusion.

*Acting*: I speak to Mrs Jones.
I post an agenda on the staffroom notice board.

*Observing*: Mrs Jones is a little hesitant because she is not clear about the brief (neither am I), but accepts provisionally. I receive three possible suggestions for inclusion on the agenda: the question of who has priority in bids for holiday timings; the state of the ladies' room; the need for flexitime. I receive two (to me) trivial suggestions about staff appearing in fancy dress in the office on Christmas Eve; and arranging for a non-smokers' room.

*Reflecting*: How can I assure Mrs Jones that she will not feel threatened?
Should I include the three sensible suggestions on the agenda, and the two trivial ones under AOB? Perhaps they are not so trivial to the staff. I am a smoker, so perhaps I do not appreciate their point of view.

The cycle continues. The manager in this office is apparently a fair-minded man, eager to be aware of the needs of his staff and to put right problems that they feel are important. It is clear that an action research approach to solving difficulties must be operated by people who are initially prepared to be sympathetic to the needs of others.

Lewin did not intend his ideas to be used in a specifically educational setting. His work made an impact in the United States and his ideas were adopted widely, at first focusing on social issues and then in education. After a decade of growth, the movement fell into decline. Carr and Kemmis (1986) identify the reasons for this growing separation of research and action, of theory and practice because of the attention paid to the booming technological industry of the 1960s. Reflecting on the work of Nevitt Sanford (1970) they say:

> As academic researchers in the social sciences began to enjoy unprecedented support from public funding bodies, they began to distinguish the work of the theorist-researcher from that of the 'engineer' responsible for putting theoretical principles into practice. The rising tide of post-Sputnik curriculum development, based on a research-development-diffusion (RD and D) model of the relationship between research and practice, legitimated and sustained this separation. . . . By the mid-1960s, (this) model had established itself as the pre-eminent model for change.
>
> (Carr and Kemmis, 1986, p. 166)

The centre of activity shifted to Britain, and the impetus now came from Lawrence Stenhouse in East Anglia.

## 2 Lawrence Stenhouse: his ideas and influence

The influence of the late Lawrence Stenhouse was crucial to the movement of action research in Britain. It was because he gave prominence to the idea of the teacher as researcher, and inspired the men and women who worked with him to develop such concepts, that the movement in Britain gained such momentum.

Stenhouse directed the Schools Council Humanities Curriculum Project from 1967 to 1972. In 1970 he moved to the University of East Anglia as director of the Centre for Applied Research in Education (CARE). The Humanities Curriculum Project aimed at establishing a liberating atmosphere for pupils in class. It emphasised the need for discussion, for close interpersonal relationships, and for the teacher to act as neutral chairman. It aimed at liberating teachers from rigid authoritarian roles.

His central message for teachers was that they should regard themselves as researchers, as the best judges of their own practice, and then the natural corollary would be an improvement of education. 'The idea is that of an educational science in which each classroom is a laboratory, each teacher a member of the scientific community,' he maintains.

> . . . All well-founded curriculum research and development, whether the work of an individual teacher, of a school, of a group working in a teachers' centre or a group working within the co-ordinating framework of a national project, is based on the study of classrooms. It thus rests on the work of teachers.

As characteristics of a professional, aware teacher he suggests:

> The commitment to systematic questioning of one's own teaching as a basis for development;
> The commitment and the skills to study one's own teaching;
> The concern to question and to test theory in practice by the use of those skills.
>
> (Stenhouse, 1975, pp. 143, 144)

At that time, however, the methods of evaluation were very much in an interpretive mode with an external researcher/observer monitoring class progress. There was still little credibility given to, or attention paid to, the interpretations by teachers of their own practice. The assumption was still that the external researcher was the expert; he ultimately wrote the reports. Teachers were there to be researched ON. Stenhouse believed that 'fruitful development in the field of curriculum and teaching depends upon evolving styles of co-operative research by teachers and using full-time researchers to support the teachers' work.' (1975, p. 162)

Stenhouse worked with people whose names are now landmarks in the literature of action research: David Hamilton, Clem Adelman, John Elliott, Barry MacDonald, Jean Rudduck, Hugh Sockett, Robert Stake, Rob Walker. These people have, through the literature and their personal influence in the field, done much to establish action research as an educational tradition (for example, Ebbutt and Elliott (1985); Rudduck and Hopkins (1985); Macdonald and Walker (1974)).

## 3 The formal schemes of Stephen Kemmis, John Elliott and Dave Ebbutt

STEPHEN KEMMIS: Currently at Deakin University, Victoria, Australia. Stephen Kemmis moved from East Anglia, where he worked with Lawrence Stenhouse, to Deakin University, Australia. He has written profusely, and has produced courses and materials on action research designed for practising teachers.

Kemmis bases his ideas on the original concept of Lewin, but he has refined it considerably. He has applied the idea exclusively to education and has, together with Wilf Carr of the University of North Wales, encouraged the use of the term 'educational action research' (1986).

Among his many excellent texts, probably the most useful for practising teachers are 'Action research' which appears in Husen and Postlethwaite's *International Encyclopedia of education: Research and studies* (1982), a succinct paper outlining principles and practice; and *The action research planner* (1982) written with Robin McTaggart, which gives detailed advice in using an action research approach to educational practices.

In the *Planner* he takes the self-reflective spiral of planning, acting, observing, reflecting, re-planning as the basis for a problem-solving manoeuvre (see Fig. 3.3).

The diagram shows the principles in action; the movement from one critical phase to another, and the way in which progress may be made through the system. An example of the system in action is (author's example):

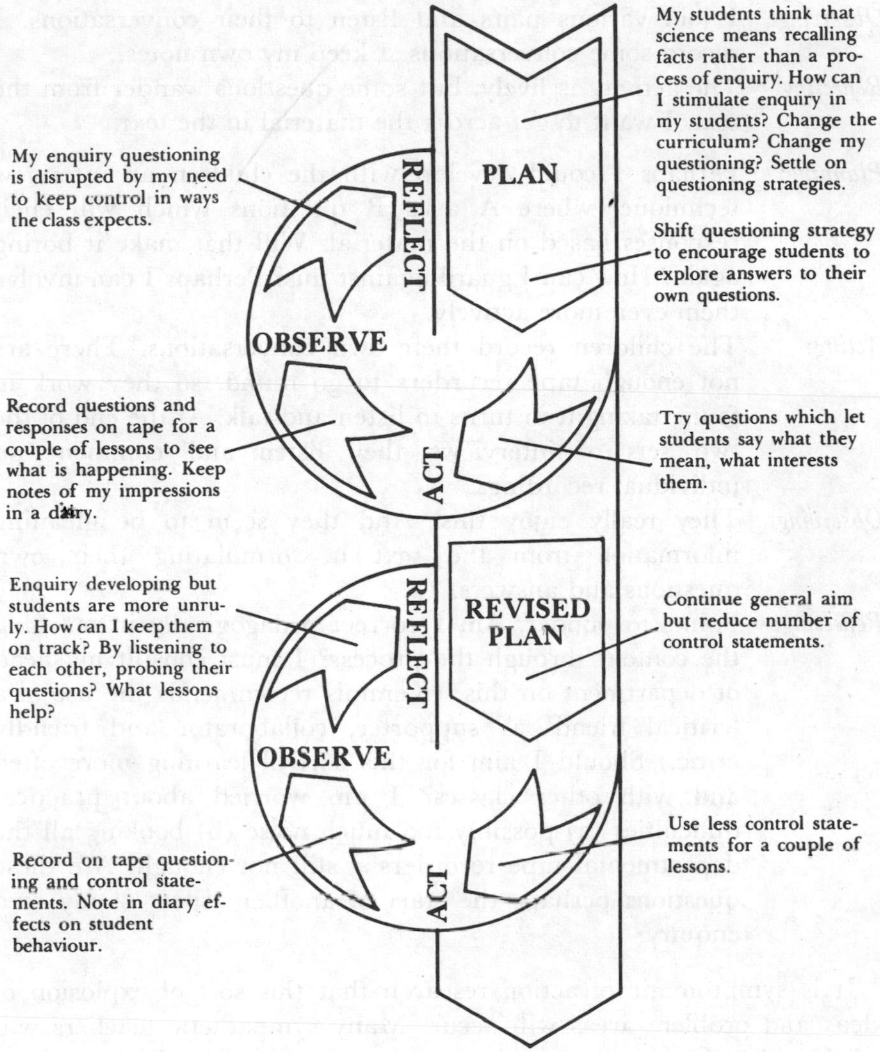
My students think that science means recalling facts rather than a process of enquiry. How can I stimulate enquiry in my students? Change the curriculum? Change my questioning? Settle on questioning strategies.
PLAN
REFLECT
My enquiry questioning is disrupted by my need to keep control in ways the class expects.
Shift questioning strategy to encourage students to explore answers to their own questions.
OBSERVE
Record questions and responses on tape for a couple of lessons to see what is happening. Keep notes of my impressions in a diary.
Try questions which let students say what they mean, what interests them.
ACT
Enquiry developing but students are more unruly. How can I keep them on track? By listening to each other, probing their questions? What lessons help?
REFLECT
REVISED PLAN
Continue general aim but reduce number of control statements.
OBSERVE
Use less control statements for a couple of lessons.
Record on tape questioning and control statements. Note in diary effects on student behaviour.
ACT

*Fig. 3.3*

*Planning*: I am not very happy with the textbook we are using, but it is the only one available. What can I do about it? I cannot change the book: should I change my method of using it? Perhaps I should try paired work.

*Acting*: I show the children how to ask and answer questions of each other to make otherwise boring material relevant to themselves.
We try out this technique in class.

*Observing*: I join various pairs and listen to their conversations. I record some conversations. I keep my own notes.

*Reflecting*: The activity is lively, but some questions wander from the text. I want to get across the material in the text.

*Planning*: Perhaps I could develop with the children an interview technique, where A asks B questions which will elicit responses based on the material. Will that make it boring again? How can I guard against this? Perhaps I can involve them even more actively.

*Acting*: The children record their own conversations. There are not enough tape recorders to go round, so they work in fours, taking it in turns to listen and talk. At the end of the two sets of interviews they listen and comment on individual recordings.

*Observing*: They really enjoy this. And they seem to be gleaning information from the text in formulating their own questions and answers.

*Reflecting*: Points to ponder: Am I correct pedagogically in teaching the content through the process? I must consult my head of department on this. (Kemmis recommends the use of a 'critical friend' as supporter, collaborator and friendly critic.) Should I aim for this sort of learning more often and with other classes? I am worried about practical difficulties (a) possibly too much noise (b) booking all the departmental tape recorders – still not enough! Are these questions perhaps the start of another aspect of my own enquiry?

It is symptomatic of action research that this sort of explosion of ideas and problem areas will occur. Many sympathetic teachers will quickly identify with the problems experienced by Zita Gisborne (see Chapter 8) in trying to cope with keeping her study going under the constraints of the practical hurly-burly of a secondary school, while still teaching a full timetable.

It is also significant that a major weakness of Kemmis's system (and others') is its supposition that life goes along only one tack at a time, forgetting that related but dissimilar problems will arise and oust the main focus, and that real people will have the flexibility and creativity to move easily to the new problem and then return to the original one. His system does not allow for such contingencies (in Fig. 3.3, for instance, what did he DO about his 'need to keep control in ways the class expects'? No further mention is made of the problem.). The argument is taken further on page 35.

Kemmis's contribution to the promotion of the ideas of action research is tremendous, and his influence has directly informed policy in Australia on the need to encourage teachers to be reflective researchers of their own practice.

JOHN ELLIOTT: Currently Professor of Education at the University of East Anglia. He worked with Lawrence Stenhouse at East Anglia, and, together with Clem Adelman, became Director of the Ford Teaching Project (1973–75). This project developed courses with the reflective teacher at their centre, and was directly in line with the thinking of Stenhouse who was then engaged in the parallel Humanities Curriculum Project. Until 1985 he was coordinator of the Classroom Action Research Network (CARN). The present coordinators are Peter Holly and Bridget Somekh.

John Elliott is an active supporter of teachers as researchers. As the coordinator of CARN, he invited educationalists from all aspects of the system, advisers and policy-makers, but particularly practising teachers, to air and share their views by contributing to the CARN bulletin and attending conferences. He is always looking for new ways to extend the network and to liaise with other action research centres and their networks.

Elliott and Adelman worked with teachers in class, not as observers, but as collaborators, in order:

1. to help teachers already attempting to implement Inquiry/ Discovery methods, but aware of a gap between attempt and achievement, to narrow this gap in their situation
2. to help teachers by fostering an action-research orientation towards classroom problems.

(Elliott and Adelman, 1973)

Through their participation they helped teachers to adopt a research approach to their work, and the literature describing projects undertaken is substantial (see, for example, Jean Rudduck, 1981, 1982; Elliott and Adelman, 1973).

Elliott agrees with the basic idea of sequential action-reflection steps running into cycles, as elaborated by Kemmis. His schema is more elaborate, however, allowing for greater fluidity between the stages, and he has produced a more refined diagram (Fig. 3.4).

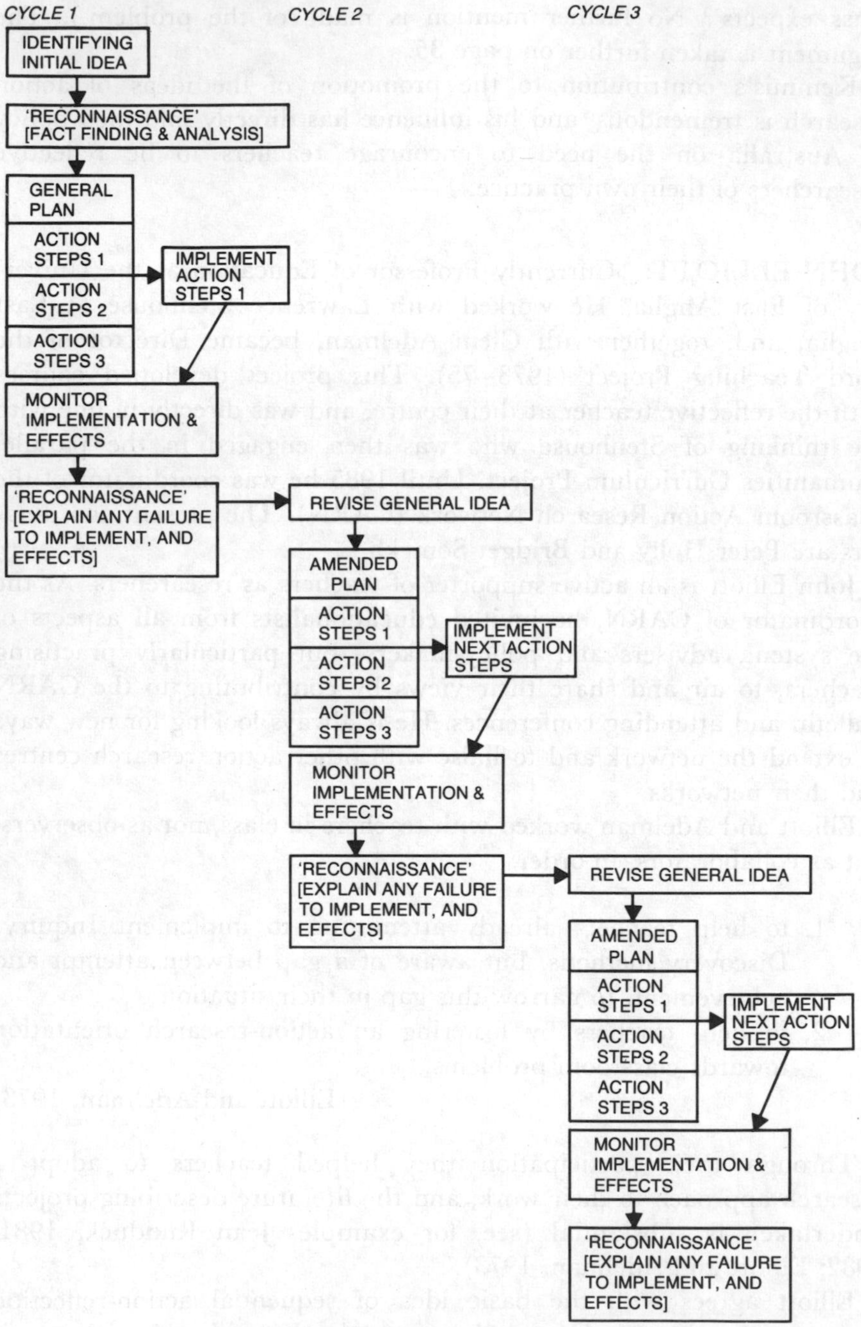
CYCLE 1
CYCLE 2
CYCLE 3
IDENTIFYING INITIAL IDEA
'RECONNAISSANCE' [FACT FINDING & ANALYSIS]
GENERAL PLAN
ACTION STEPS 1
ACTION STEPS 2
ACTION STEPS 3
IMPLEMENT ACTION STEPS 1
MONITOR IMPLEMENTATION & EFFECTS
'RECONNAISSANCE' [EXPLAIN ANY FAILURE TO IMPLEMENT, AND EFFECTS]
REVISE GENERAL IDEA
AMENDED PLAN
ACTION STEPS 1
ACTION STEPS 2
ACTION STEPS 3
IMPLEMENT NEXT ACTION STEPS
MONITOR IMPLEMENTATION & EFFECTS
'RECONNAISSANCE' [EXPLAIN ANY FAILURE TO IMPLEMENT, AND EFFECTS]
REVISE GENERAL IDEA
AMENDED PLAN
ACTION STEPS 1
ACTION STEPS 2
ACTION STEPS 3
IMPLEMENT NEXT ACTION STEPS
MONITOR IMPLEMENTATION & EFFECTS
'RECONNAISSANCE' [EXPLAIN ANY FAILURE TO IMPLEMENT, AND EFFECTS]

*Fig 3.4*

DAVE EBBUTT: Currently Senior Research Officer, Homerton Educational Research and Development Unit, Cambridge, and a colleague and collaborator of John Elliott.

Dave Ebbutt agrees basically with the ideas of Kemmis and Elliott, but disagrees about some of Elliott's interpretations of Kemmis's work. He comments (1983):

> It seems clear to me that Elliott is wrong in one respect, in suggesting that Kemmis equates reconnaissance with fact finding only. The Kemmis diagram clearly shows reconnaissance to comprise discussing, negotiating, exploring opportunities, assessing possibilities and examining constraints – in short there are elements of analysis in the Kemmis notion of reconnaissance. Nevertheless I suggest that the thrust of Elliott's three statements is an attempt on the part of a person experienced in directing action research projects to recapture some of the 'messiness' of the action research cycle which the Kemmis version tends to gloss.

Further, he claims that the spiral is not the most useful way in which to describe the action-reflection process. Instead he offers the following diagram (Fig. 3.5).

In his recent work Ebbutt has shown that he is concerned with the logic of action research. He points out the essential difference between theorising about systems, and putting those systems into operation in real life:

> I had made the assumption that Elliott's logic and Kemmis's maxims were being used synonymously to describe the same thing. But as I now understand it, maxims are little more than rule of thumb, or rules of the art. Maxim tells us something about successfully operationalizing action research but it does not determine the practice of action research. Maxim has been derived empirically by successful practitioners of action research, whereas the logic of action research determines the practice upon which they came to engage.
>
> (Ebbutt, 1985)

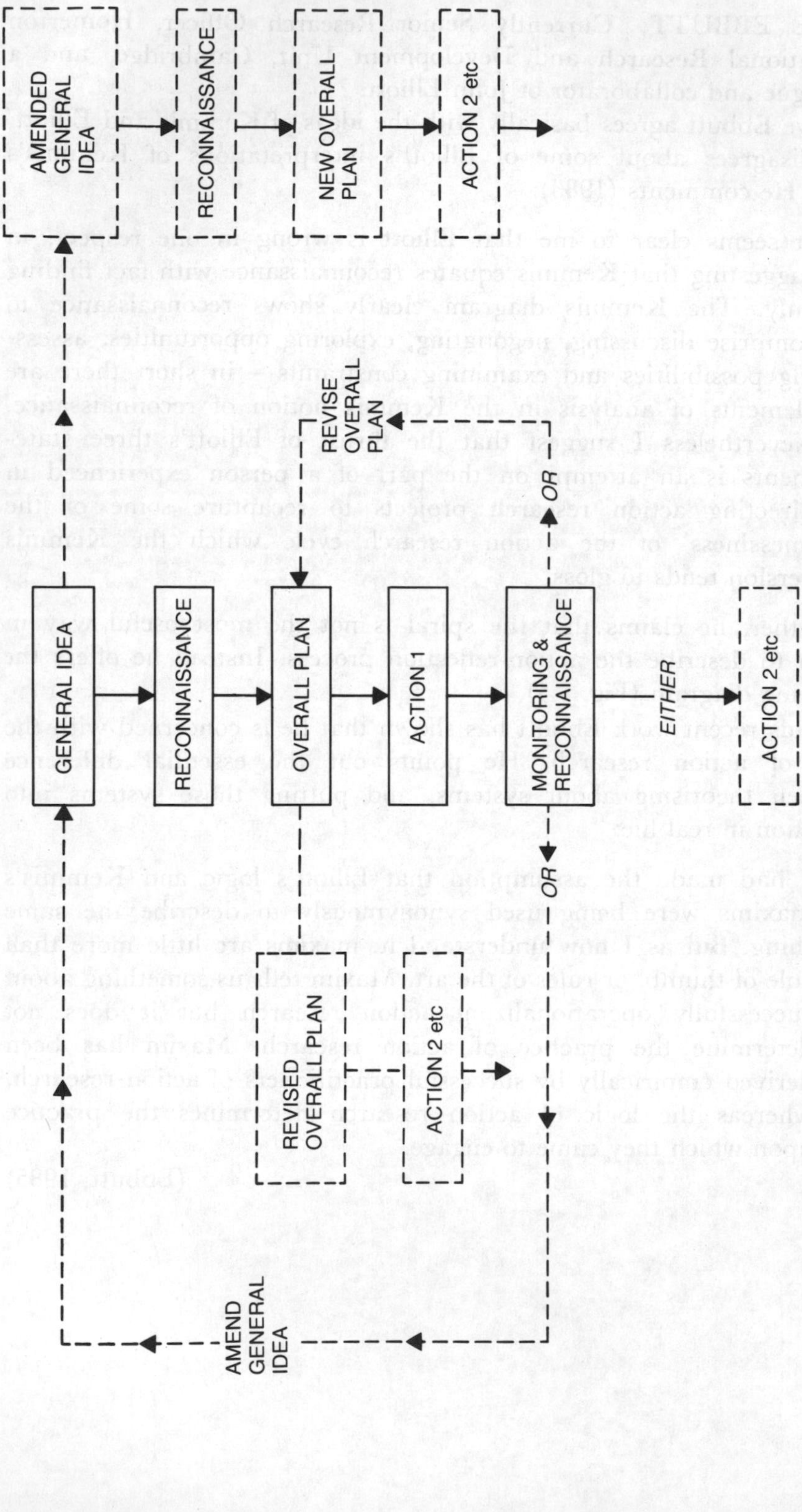


*Fig. 3.5* *Idealized Representation of the Process of Action Research*

*Comment on the work of Kemmis, Elliott and Ebbutt*

There are four significant points in the schemes of Kemmis, Elliott and Ebbutt that need careful attention by teachers planning to apply the schemes to their class practice. These points are not necessarily criticisms, for the schemes are useful in the way their authors intended. Teachers should be aware, however, of the uses and possible limitation of the schemes in practice. The points are:

1 There is movement away from Lewin's original notions.
2 The schemes tend to be rigid and confusing.
3 They cannot deal with novel situations within the main focus.
4 They are not in themselves educational.

These points are expanded:

1 Lewin originally saw action research as a way of describing professional development in social situations. It came later to be applied to what teacher–researchers were doing, particularly in the work of Corey (1953) (see page 19). Kemmis, Elliott and Ebbutt seem to have moved away from this notion in that their schemes have become prescriptive rather than descriptive, observational rather than explanatory (see point 2). Certainly research workers and authors in other disciplines borrow terms and apply them to their own work, but it is important here to remember that Lewin's original concept might have formed the basis, but does not appear to be the practice, of the work identified so far. Hopkins notes (1985):

> Recently, much energy has been misplaced because Lewin's conception of action research is very different from what goes on in the name of teacher research. Lewin's concept of action research was (i) as an externally initiated intervention designed to assist a client system, (ii) functionalist in orientation, and (iii) prescriptive in practice. None of these features apply to what I assume to be the nature of classroom research by teachers which is characterized by its practitioner, problem solving, and eclectic orientation.

Kemmis himself notes (1982) that his concept of action research has moved significantly from the earlier notions of Lewin, and Carr and Kemmis (1986) have turned the concept into the basis for 'an adequate and coherent educational science'.

Hopkins (1985) is also worried about the values inherent in Lewin's ideas.

The functionalist values that appear in his writing tend to offset his commitment to democratic and communitarian values. It is doubly ironic that Kemmis illustrates the process of action research by citing Lewin's example of the bombing of German factories!

2 At the beginning of this chapter, the point was made that the word 'model' implied a prescriptive element, a rigidity of design and purpose that denied the spontaneity and creativity that is characteristic of life in classrooms. There is a danger that the systems discussed so far could be seen in this light for at least three reasons.

First, there is a need to look at functional levels. This idea makes the point that in any enquiry there are at least three such levels, those of observation, description and explanation (see Chomsky, 1965; McNiff, 1984). An enquiry may observe (note what is happening), describe (tell what is happening) and explain (say why and how it is happening). It seems that the systems of Kemmis, Elliott and Ebbutt stop short at the levels of observation and description. They do not attempt to explain the educational phenomena they are dealing with, and therefore they cannot be said to be truly educational. Hopkins notes (1985) that 'the models . . . delineate a sequence of stages, but say little about the "what" and "how" within these stages.' Perhaps the most telling criticism against these researchers who claim to be action researchers is that they do not make a claim to account for their own personal and professional development. They do not, in fact, map their own imagined frameworks onto their own practice. Instead of attempting to demonstrate the marriage of their own theory and practice, and the demolition of the distinction between research and pedagogy, they tend to present abstract systems in which theory comes first and practice follows on.

Second, because the systems do not have this built-in explanatory power, they might tend to be prescriptive, that is, tell teachers what to do rather than indicate possible ways of how to do it. The systems themselves are intended to work on a 'how to do' basis, as a means to follow through any educational enquiry, but the very style in which the 'how to do' advice is couched leads to a 'what to do' approach. Teachers who use the systems as a means of solving their own classroom problems may find in dismay that they cannot fit themselves and their practice into the tightly structured frameworks and, as one notable commentator pointed out in the preparation of this manuscript, 'one might argue that some of the finest classroom enquiries have developed along very different lines (for example,

Armstrong, 1980; and Rowland, 1984)', which are NOT examples of action research.

Third, the schemes appear confusing and therefore daunting. In their efforts to portray a stylised reality, the authors have opted for systems resting on an intellectual basis, and the visual representations reflect this mental reality rather than class reality. Even Ebbutt admits that he finds Elliott's schema mystifying (1983), while Hopkins comments (1985): 'What began as a useful label to describe a loose set of activities undertaken for professional development purposes is in danger of assuming a rather different character as a result of a quest for intellectual credibility.'

3 When I first started my own research study I had a naive view of the nature of problems in education. I tended to think that having once identified a problem I could work towards its solution, on a once-and-for-all basis. Having been resolved, the problem was a closed book. My practice showed me that this was far from the truth. I seemed no sooner to have reached some sort of solution for one problem than another set arose in its place, rather like the Hydra. The more I investigated the problems of my own class practice, the more I became aware that observable problems of, say, misbehaviour, were symptoms of deeper, underlying problems. The more I attempted to work towards solutions, the more it seemed I was forced to break off from the main focus of my enquiry, and deal with other, equally significant aspects. I found at first that I was quite confused as to what constituted my main enquiry, how many of the 'subsidiary' problem areas I should attend to and in what detail, and what sort of research design I could adopt to give the whole scientific rigour and help me to cope. Zita Gisborne (Case study 2, Chapter 8) had the same difficulties of selection, focus, and keeping one's head above water while trying to be a researcher as well as an everyday class teacher!

The systems of Kemmis, Elliott and Ebbutt simply do not accommodate spontaneous, creative episodes. On page 28 I wondered how Kemmis dealt with the problem of unrest in class that he wrote in the formal schedule. Did he return to it? solve it? abandon it? In my own work I am attempting to formulate a theory to explain my own way of dealing with this problem (see page 45) but it is a significant aspect that so far has not been dealt with satisfactorily in the literature.

4 Perhaps the gravest shortcoming in the schemes is that they are not intrinsically educational. While it is true that they deal with

matters of education, their use does not encourage teachers to account for their own personal development; that is, to offer explanations of how and why they have been prompted to change their practice, and to demonstrate publicly that this change has led to an improvement. To return to the ideas of Stenhouse for a moment of comparison: he postulated a two-tier educational classroom system: that because the curriculum stressed the importance of process as much as content (for example, the ability to talk about a subject as well as knowledge of the subject area itself) pupils were involved on a personal basis, and the process of their education was enhanced. At the second level, because the style of teaching this curriculum allowed teachers to become aware and critical of their own practice, that is, enquiring practitioners, the process of their education also was enhanced. The schemes of Kemmis, Elliott and Ebbutt require teachers only to apply systems to their pupils. In this sense they may be accused of prescriptivism and possibly even of being no further advanced in educational democracy than an interpretive tradition.

The allegation of lack of educational contribution is compounded if we consider that the schemes are propositional in character rather than practical, that is that they make statements on paper without showing in practice how those statements are realised in the reality of their own and other people's lives. The schemes, their descriptions and functions are communicated in words only. Now this may be that the greatest communication channel is via the printed word, and that the reader is then called upon to interpret the written word into a whole reality. But the authors do not specifically require teachers to give explanations for their own personal involvement, nor do they show how they have 'come to know' why they make the statements they do, nor defend their claim to knowledge. They have produced elegant word diagrams on paper, disagreeing among themselves on matters of linguistics, mostly semantics, that is, what words and their functions mean, without actually giving a substance to the form.

What is needed is an educational component – action that will turn the form into reality. Just as an actor takes words written on paper (the form of a play) and turns it into life (the substance); just as a speaker takes the form of language (phonemes, sounds, pauses) and turns them into meanings (intentional utterances); so a teacher takes a form of research (the schemes of Kemmis, Elliott and Ebbutt) and tries to turn them into a real improvement of practice. It is not that the schemes are faulty; it is that they are deficient. They do not have the explanatory power to enable teachers to generate their own educational theory from their own educational practice.

So I now turn to work that has been going on in Bath, and in particular the ideas of Jack Whitehead, who aims to work towards an educational research tradition by offering explanations for his own educational practices and by inviting other teacher–researchers to do the same.

## 4 Jack Whitehead and his notion of a living educational theory

JACK WHITEHEAD: Currently a Lecturer in Education at the University of Bath. He has published extensively, and has been instrumental in setting up action research networks in the south west of Britain.

He feels that Kemmis, Elliott and Ebbutt are in danger of moving away from the reality of educational practice. He is keen to keep the teacher–practitioner at the centre of the enquiry. Unless we keep the living 'I' in our educational discussions, he maintains, action research loses touch with reality and becomes an academic exercise. He stresses the importance of this notion, saying that the 'I' of each individual is his unassailable and inalienable integrity, and that the 'I' is a living, pro-active entity. It is vital that we acknowledge the force of the individual consciousness in interpersonal relationships. It is this force that makes possible, and its acknowledgement that encourages, a one-to-one relationship between persons that is fundamental to human enquiry.

He maintains that the focus of educational research should be

> to improve the relationship between educational theory and professional development. We take educational theory to be a kind of theory which can arise from, and, in turn, generate explanations for the educational development of individuals in a form which is open to public testing.
>
> (Whitehead and Foster, 1984)

Whitehead became interested in action research as a reaction to the 1960s influence of Peters and Hirst and the disciplines approach to educational research. He worked with a small group of teachers centred on Bath, using an approach that suggested that improvements in class were sustained by the teachers' self-evaluation of the differences between their ideas and their practice.

> What began as a modest attempt to understand how a small group of teachers worked to improve their practice has grown over the past decade into an integrated approach to professional development which uses action research to generate an educational theory which can be directly related to educational practice.
>
> (Whitehead, 1986)

In order to make action research meaningful to the lives of real, individual educators, he has re-formulated the action-reflection cycle into a pattern of statements. These statements act as a general formula for tackling practical educational problems in a systematic way. They are:

1 I experience a problem when some of my educational values are denied in practice (for example, My pupils do not seem to be taking as active a part in my lessons as I would want them to).
2 I imagine a solution to the problem. (Should I organise my lessons so that my pupils have to ask questions? Shall I try group work, or structured exercises?)
3 I implement the imagined solution. (I try group work as from Tuesday's lesson, and I introduce structured worksheets that lead my pupils to ask and answer questions without my constant supervision.)
4 I evaluate the outcome of my actions. (Yes, my pupils are certainly participating more, but they are making too much noise. Also, they are still depending on me in the form of worksheets.)
5 I re-formulate my problem in the light of my evaluation. (I must find a way of persuading them to be involved but less noisy. I must find a way to make them more independent of me in their own educational development.)

The thrust of Jack Whitehead's argument is that action research must of itself be educational. It must help teachers try to make sense of their normal, everyday practice.

This action-reflection spiral is a basis for teacher self-improvement. It can be tied in with a set of questions which act as a starting point to curriculum reform:

1 What is your concern?
2 Why are you concerned?
3 What do you think you could do about it?

4 What kind of 'evidence' could you collect to help you make some judgement about what is happening?
5 How would you collect such 'evidence'?
6 How could you check that your judgement about what has happened is reasonably fair and accurate?

There are many current initiatives which follow such patterns. A small selection includes: the work of Ronald King at City of Bath College of Further Education, Pam Lomax at Kingston Polytechnic, Denis Vincent at North East London Polytechnic, George Preston and Joan Whitehead at Bath College of Higher Education, Michael Bassey at Trent Polytechnic (see also Bassey (1986)), David Hustler at Manchester Polytechnic; Bulmershe College, Reading, runs an MEd in Classroom Studies; Bristol Polytechnic and Bath College of Higher Education run a diploma in professional studies by action research; Sheffield Polytechnic has an MEd course by action enquiry. (See also Chapter 10.) A number of individual teachers, notably in Avon and Wiltshire, are engaged in a systematic process of curriculum review and evaluation. The number of institutions which are incorporating an enquiry in action approach is growing rapidly.

It would be inconsistent to suppose that the essence of this form of a living educational theory could be communicated only through these words on paper. A growing number of colleagues and students are developing the approach through their accounts of their own educational lives in their Higher Degree dissertations, their published reports and books (for example, Eames, 1987; Larter, 1987; Jensen, 1987; Joan Whitehead, 1987; McNiff, 1986) as well as through the live networks that are in existence and expanding. Real people are the best theory; the most effective way of explaining ideas is to show what they mean in action.

What this group of researchers are finding (Lomax, 1986; Lomax and Whitehead, 1987) is that they have to acknowledge the importance of dialogue in their educational development. For example, they are exploring ways of presenting their accounts in terms of dialogues such as the one below between a teacher and lecturers from Further and Higher Education, as they viewed a video tape of the teacher's practice.

*Personnel*: Mike (teacher in an 11–18 comprehensive school); Ron (lecturer in further education); Mary and Jack (lecturers in the School of Education, University of Bath).

The dialogue moves us through Mike's expression of commitment to the value of promoting an environment in which pupils will put forward their own point of view, to Mary's judgement that his practice encourages conformity.

*Mike*: I mentioned cooperation. Certainly that would involve group work in pairs or in larger groups. I'm very concerned about competitiveness that is attached, for example, to marks that are given out to work and I'd like to find ways to break that down. In the first years I don't actually put marks on the work the students produce. I put comments. I put marks in the mark book.

So many values include cooperation through group work, lack of competitiveness, the willingness of individuals within the group to put forward their own point of view rather than feel they have to shy away from making a comment because it may be negated by other people . . .

*Mary*: At the moment the geography of the school classroom inhibits any real relationship developing between the pupils . . . Mike can't really achieve his values of cooperation between the students while they are all looking at someone else's back. Mike can only do what he does, which is why presumably he does it. You have been put in the position over the years of perfecting this mode.

I think there is a very important place for what you do, but if that is the whole diet of the kids in every lesson in the school they are going to come out deskilled because they never have to take the responsibility for asking a question.

*Mike*: I accept that. The thing that is interesting about that is whether other people would see that as a problem.

*Mary*: I'm sure they wouldn't.

*Mike*: Lots of people would look at that and say that is very very good indeed and wouldn't go further than that.

*Mary*: It's true. You have got attention. You are clear. It's structured. It's excellent. But if your values are to promote the ethical . . .

*Jack*: Go through the values, Mary.

*Mary*: To promote a moral awareness, to promote a spirit of harmony, of cooperation, of respect, of students listening to each other which cannot happen at the moment because of the arrangement and you cannot promote these values easily. What you can promote is a conformity, listening to the teacher, responding to what the teacher is provoking or prompting, and they learn that skill very well in school.

*Mike*: I'm interested in what you said about conformity.

*Mary*: It must do it. They are all acting as a class. It must do because you are calling the shots from the front.

*Ron*: They learn it very well, too. They come to our college and they behave in an exemplary fashion. They sit in rows for two hours at a time. They don't respond. They are passive. It's a terrible job to break this down.

*Mary*: How do you break this down in the sixth form?

*Mike*: Having small groups helps. I have a group of four in my upper sixth. It means with a small number everybody participates.

*Mary*: That's it. That is why I was pressing you to break the class into groups.

Dialogue and the building of dialogical communities (Bernstein, 1983) must be a primary focus of educational intent. Propositions are not enough. We must talk about the propositions and strive to reach common understandings.

This approach to establishing educational communities based on dialogue is crucial to the Whitehead philosophy. Dialogue consists of question and answer, and the logic of question and answer is also known as dialectical logic. In dialectics the focus is on change which will move, not oust or supplant, another point of view, including one's own. It results in metamorphosis rather than restructuring.

For example, consider the well-known Yin Yang diagram (Fig. 3.6):

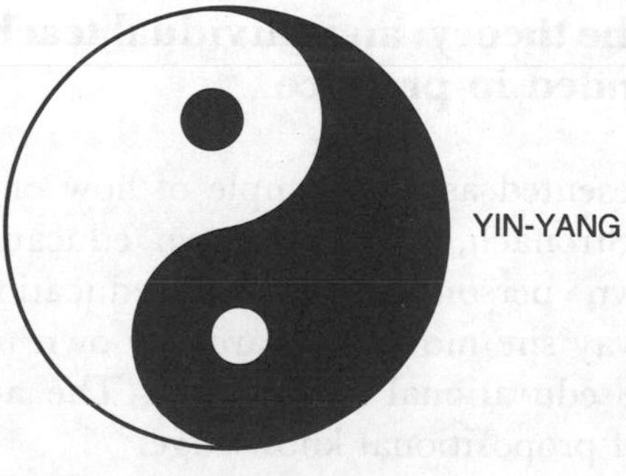


*Fig. 3.6*

If one portion moves it alters its own shape and that of its companion. There are no empty spaces. Each entity is in flux with the other, accommodating the other to itself without losing its original identity. Consider also that each has something of the other inside itself (the dot of its partner's colour), indicating that both are mutually dependent for their existence.

So it is in dialectics. One question becomes another's answer; the answer in turn becomes a question. It is a dance of communication. Questions for educators mean carefully considering practice – 'What am I doing?' 'Why am I doing it?' – and these questions give a living form to an educational enquiry. The practitioner is living out his questions, and his tentative answers to those questions make his own personal theory.

Life is not static. Answers and questions will change, as will focus, perspective, and the living form of the individual who is formulating them. In this way his personal and professional life is organic, and his personal theories of education also. He will develop theories which account for his practice as and when that practice occurs, and his stimulus for, and approach to, the process of change will be a consideration for others which is grounded in question and answer.

By the same token this book may be seen in its propositional sense, that is of words on paper, organised to make sense and communicate a meaning. But the best way of communicating in order to improve educational practices is to contact the reality. One of the purposes of this book is to stimulate you into doing something about your own practice, and perhaps you will identify with some of the concerns expressed by the other teachers mentioned here.

## 5 Advancing the theory: an individual teacher as a maker of theory grounded in practice

This section is presented as an example of how one practitioner may 'come to know' (Stronach, 1986) her own educational practice, and formulate her own personal theory of education based on that practice. In this way she moves forward her own understandings and contributes to the educational community. The account aims to go beyond the level of propositional knowledge.

From 1974 to 1987 I was deputy headmistress at a secondary school in Bournemouth, and from 1981 a part-time research student at the University of Bath.

In my own study I have taken an action-enquiry approach in my attempt to understand my own educational practices and my efforts to improve the quality of education for the people in my care. In the early stages of my work I was much attracted by the systems of Kemmis and Elliott, but I soon found them wanting in two major respects: they did not reflect the reality of my professional life and its random hurly-burly nature; and therefore they did not give me an opportunity to explain why and how my life took this form. In this respect I felt that to follow their schemes to the letter would have been prescriptive rather than educational, rather like University A on page xv who wanted to lead me rather than walk with me.

I developed, among others, two major themes in my work: the need for explanatory adequacy in educational research and the need for a theory with generative capacity, that is, that could communicate the potential of one theory to create new theories. Rather than stopping at the traditional notion of a theory arising out of a specific set of circumstances and having relevance only to that setting, a generative approach views a theory as an organic device to create other theories that may be applied in other settings.

As a student of linguistics I was attracted to the notion of adequacy as developed by Noam Chomsky (1965). He suggested three levels of adequacy: observational, descriptive, and explanatory. I had already rejected the disciplines approach as a basis for my enquiry in that it stopped short at the descriptive level; I went on to reject the alternative models of Kemmis and Elliott on the same charge.

I felt that there was a need for a theory with generative capacity to allow for spontaneous, creative episodes. Human systems rest on the notion that a finite number of components are capable of producing an infinite number of novel phenomena. For example, a grammar contains a finite number of elements which in use may produce an infinite number of original utterances; a fixed number of mathematical principles – adding, multiplying, subtracting, dividing – can account for an infinite number of computations; a fixed number of facial components – eyes, nose, mouth, etc. – can produce an infinite number of unique faces; one acorn holds within itself its own generative power to become an oak tree. Research should have this same self-generative capacity.

The spirals of planning, acting, observing, reflecting, re-planning, in the frameworks presented so far are able to deal with only one problem at a time. Action research should offer the capacity to deal with a number of problems at the same time by allowing the spirals to develop spin-off spirals, just as in reality one problem will be symptomatic of many other underlying problems.

For example, the problem identified in Kemmis's diagram (Fig. 3.3) is one of stimulating enquiry in the students. Kemmis observes that, 'My enquiry questioning is disrupted by my need to keep control in ways the class expects', an equally serious educational problem, yet it is abandoned within the plan. A generative framework accommodates it.

In Fig. 3.7 the central column is the main issue. It follows the Kemmis/Elliott/Whitehead action-reflection spiral, except that visually it is now three-dimensional.

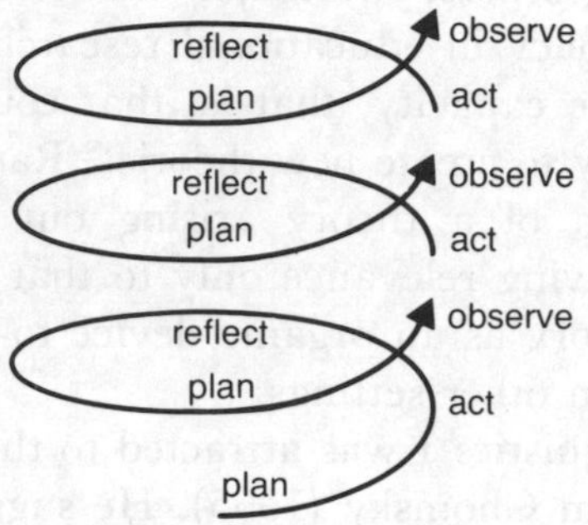


*Fig. 3.7*

Add to the main column an action-reflection cycle to follow through the problem of class control (Fig. 3.8).

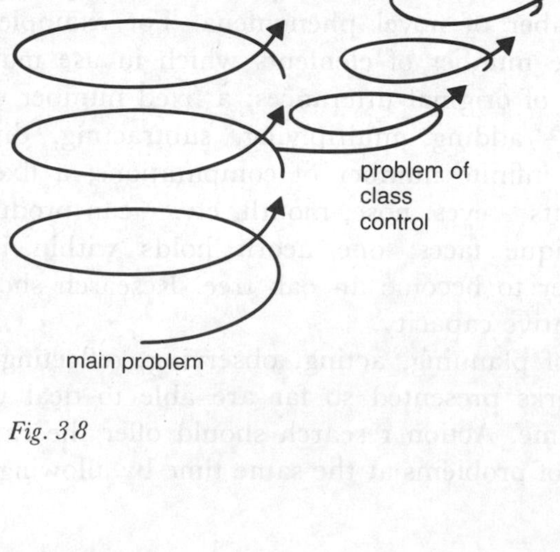


*Fig. 3.8*

Other problems may be explored as and when they arise without the researcher losing sight of the main focus of the enquiry. The visual which would reflect the action is a three-dimensional spiral of spirals (Fig. 3.9).

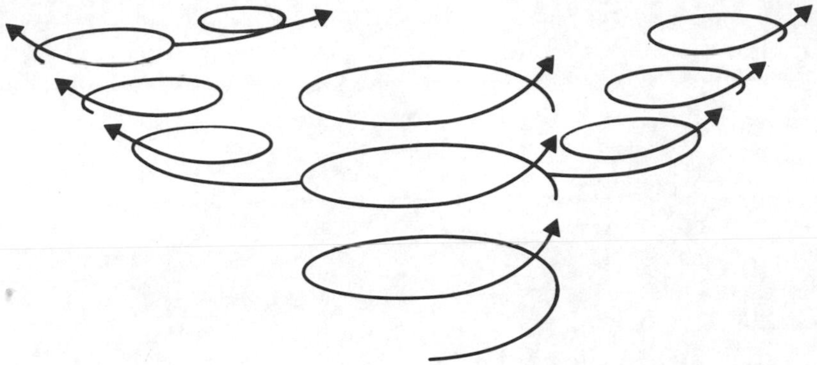

*Fig 3.9*

These ideas have been used by some of my fellow researchers at Bath as a device to enter an enquiry at any point with other questions of concern, and to follow those questions through to a satisfactory conclusion.

Generative action research enables a teacher–researcher to address many different problems at one time without losing sight of the main issue. For example, in his investigation into his practice in PE, David M. was concerned with the general lack of motivation among fifth-formers in sport. In adopting an action-enquiry mode to his problem, he interviewed a number of boys, but found that they were hostile to his personal approach. Before he could tackle the main issue he had to find ways of combating the hostility and establishing an atmosphere of trust. His research reports show that, in fact, his then secondary issue turned into a primary issue; he discovered that the lack of trust and personal ease between staff and pupils was a principal contributory factor in the lack of interest in sport, or, indeed, in many areas of school life. By adopting a formative approach to his work, and building in to his personal methodology the facility of switching focus while maintaining a systematic, disciplined enquiry, David was able to meet the needs of his pupils; and his understanding of their development and his own ability, through reflective enquiry, to assist that development, led to an enhancement of his own personal and professional education.

This chapter has briefly outlined the state of the art. The ideas presented serve only as signposts. They are not static, but in a constant state of revision as their creators move forward in their own educational enquiries.

# Chapter 4

# Why Teachers Should Engage in Action Research

## Introduction

Teachers may benefit considerably by taking a close, critical look at their own practice. Developed and refined insights as to the nature of that practice, professional autonomy and competence, and authority to give a reasoned justification for their own educational work may result. The concept 'educational' involves the notion of 'improvement'. By being aware and critical of their practice, teachers work more positively towards their own professional development. The mood is right for action research in the teaching profession. This is seen in at least three ways: political, professional, personal.

## Political

The 1980s have seen an increased focus on the teacher as a central manager of education. Much attention has recently been paid to school-based curriculum development and research-based in-service education. Current thinking encourages schools to identify their own needs and initiate actions to meet those needs. For example, the Open University 'Curriculum in action' evaluation pack adopts a step-by-step procedure to recognise the everyday practicalities of a real class situation. The steps are in the form of questions:

1 What did the children do?
2 What were they learning?
3 How worthwhile was it?

and then, inviting the teacher to be critical of her own practice:

4 What did I, the teacher, do?

5 What did I learn?
6 What do I intend to do now?

By adopting this plan teachers can work individually and collaboratively to make sense of their own educational situations.

With mid-1980s initiatives (for example, TVEI and injections of funds for in-service training) there is an emphasis on a real need for schools to be responsible for their own curriculum research and development, and for the necessary and appropriate in-service support. Such importance is attached to this view that the whole notion of funding has changed. Broadly speaking, instead of funds being allocated at county or regional level, individual schools now bid for funding for their own particular identified need. So, for example, School A might feel that they need to enhance the quality of science education in the school. They will put in a bid to their LEA for funding for, for example, the county adviser or an independent agent to visit the school for extra support; or they might request, in collaboration with other schools in the area, for the local teachers' centre to put on a course which will cover their area of need. The system is school-based, practitioner-centred in-service education.

Many schools' curricula are not only content based, but also skills and attitudes based. Teaching skills and competencies are needed that perhaps were not catered for in most initial teacher training schemes, and these competencies are of a more personal and social nature. The development of these skills cannot come about through the vicarious experience of taught courses or knowledge-based schemes of work. This development is personal. It comes about as a process of experiencing, and being aware and critical of that experiencing.

For example, Mary G. found in her teaching of geography that she was moving away from a fact base – capital cities, rivers, mountain ranges, rainfalls – to a social base – environmental factors, pollution, conservation, population rates. The shift in content demanded from her a shift in teaching style and approach to the subject. She not only had to be in command of her subject matter; she also had to explore her own attitudes to social, economic and political factors. She had to be prepared to present her material in such a way that she was assisting her children's awareness of these issues through the subject matter.

This discussion highlights alternative views of the nature of education itself, whether it is a commodity or a process. The notion of education as a commodity is essentially political, that is, has to do with power and who is wielding that power. It is a view that says the person who has power has the most of everything, including the most of education. Education becomes a desirable STUFF, like money or property or clothes. If this is a prevailing attitude, teachers will be caught up in the net. The end product of their work will be functional, utilitarian, geared towards perpetuating a society that is founded on possessions, and believes that wealthy is healthy. This seems still to be a prevailing attitude in many areas of our educational system.

An alternative view of education as process was given substance in Stenhouse's Humanities Curriculum Project. The nature of the educational endeavour was one of being rather than having (see also Fromm, 1978). Many projects aimed at increasingly personal, social and moral competence are geared towards this philosophy (for example, Kohlberg, 1976; Button, 1981, 1982; Baldwin and Wells, 1979, 1980, 1981. For reviews of this area, see Pring, 1984; McNiff, 1986).

Mary Warnock sums up (1977) that education is '. . . *essentially* something which must be tailored to its recipient; . . . it . . . must come from the pupil himself' and the task of educators is to '. . . make sure that this growth is not inhibited, or that it is, more positively, encouraged'.

## Professional

In their excellent book *Becoming critical* (1986) Wilf Carr and Stephen Kemmis define the character of a profession. It has for them three distinctive features;

> . . . that professions employ methods and procedures based on theoretical knowledge and research; . . . that the members of the profession have an overriding commitment to the well-being of their clients; . . . that, individually and collectively, the members of the profession reserve the right to make autonomous and independent judgments, free from external non-professional controls and constraints, about the particular courses of action to be adopted in any particular situation. Emancipatory action research suggests an image of the teaching profession which incorporates these features in a distinctive way.

If teaching is to be regarded as a profession, then teachers must be prepared to employ methods and procedures based on theoretical research and knowledge. Action research provides a method whereby they can themselves develop this research and knowledge, for testing and improving their own classroom practice, and for establishing a sound rationale for what they are doing. Built in to action research is the proviso that, if as a teacher I am dissatisfied with what is already going on, I will have the confidence and resolution to attempt to change it. I will not be content with the status quo, but I will have a sound foundation of personal knowledge to enable me to change the direction of my life and that of the children in my care. So, if marking seems to be taking every spare moment of my life, and I am unhappy about the situation, I will explore ways and means to reduce the quantity and enhance the quality of my own life as a person and a teacher; if my pupils seem restless in my German lessons because they still do not understand case endings, then I will actively explore the situation to help them understand and enhance the quality of their education; if my links with our Educational Welfare Officer are too tenuous, then I will look at ways to strengthen them. At all levels of my school life I can assess unsatisfactory situations in a level-headed way, make clear decisions about what needs to be done to improve the situations, try them out, and change them again if they do not work; but all this in a systematic and public way, in collaboration with other colleagues and with the people involved – pupils, my head of department, the Educational Welfare Officer. Together we explore the options, and together we all benefit.

The second criterion, that of commitment to clients, has intense implications for the politics and ethics of teaching. For being committed to something suggests a thinking awareness. If I am not committed I do not care. If I am committed, then I am acutely aware, and I question. If I do not question, I accept the status quo, and I go along with established systems and attitudes without interfering. I am a servant of the system, and I service it through my passivity.

Teachers do not do this, not teachers engaged in action research, trying to understand and improve their educational situation. Acquiescence is not a characteristic of an action researcher. He is resourceful, committed, tenacious, and above all curious. He will not be satisfied with a given system if he sees elements of the system as unsatisfactory. He will seek to change it. In so doing, he refuses to be a servant, but becomes an acting agent. He rises above the role of skilled technician and becomes an educator. And this qualifies him to meet the third criterion, of being able to make autonomous and independent judgements within his own professional sphere. By adopting a thinking, critical attitude towards his own practice, and testing his research findings against public opinion, he will be qualified to give reasoned justifications for his actions.

The idea of technician versus actor is a vigorous theme in the writings of Aristotle. He made the point that a service mode is one of 'techne', that is mastering and applying techniques, whereas 'praxis' is a wise and considered practice.

> For neither is acting a way of making – nor making a way of truly acting. Architecture (techne) is a way of making . . . of bringing something into being whose origin is in the maker and not in the thing. Making has always an end other than itself, action not; for good action itself is its end. Perfection in making is an art, perfection in acting is a virtue.
>
> (*Nichomachean Ethics*)

In my opinion, to expect teachers to accept the status quo, to do as they are told, is to relegate them to a service role of technicians. To qualify as real educators, teachers must be given the strongest encouragement to apply their wisdom, gained through long and strenuous experience, in their praxis. Education is not a business of manufacturing. It is literally a growth area, for pupils and teachers alike. Once teachers embark on the journey of self-education, then thinking becomes action, and action becomes a never-ending cycle of re-creation.

## Personal

I like to believe I was a good teacher before I embarked on my own research project. I did not actively start to think systematically about what I was doing, however, until I was fifteen years into teaching, when I became an action researcher and, in consequence, independent of previous constraints. These constraints were usually in the form of other people's expectations of me. My colleagues, my headteachers, my pupils, all expected me to fit into some kind of predetermined mould, and I felt I had to live up to that image. All that changed through my study. Like Jennifer Nias (1984) I came to see that I was an autonomous person as well as a functional teacher, and I strove to balance 'the deeply held values and attitudes of the substantial self and the behaviour expected by significant others of the situational self'. I see my children now as thinking persons, independent of me. I see life through their eyes, and I am quicker to judge myself than to judge them. I am a humane teacher rather than a clever operator, because I have become a thinking person. Pam Lomax (1986) points out that Revans puts it neatly (1980): 'The clever man will tell you what he knows; he may even try to explain it to you. The wise man encourages you to discover it for yourself, even though he knows it inside out.'

This book adopts the same attitude. It cannot instruct teachers to engage in action research. That would be dictatorial, reverting to a positivist stand of 'I know what is best for you, so you must do it'. It cannot identify the personal, idiosyncratic problem areas of personal practice. Only a practising teacher can do that, for she is immediately and intensively involved in the creativity of her own class situation (see Chapter 1 in Ebbutt and Elliott, 1985.)

Thinking is an adventure. It becomes a journey towards self-knowledge. It is inherently hazardous, for thinking implies change, and change is usually uncomfortable. Yet, as Michael Polanyi says (1958, pp. 314, 327), '. . . in spite of the hazards involved, I am called upon to search for truth and state my findings. . . . I must understand the world from my point of view, as a person claiming originality and exercising his judgment responsibly and with universal intent.' (Polanyi's premise is further investigated on page 133).

It is this claim to knowledge that action research makes possible, but such knowledge cannot be gained through passive acceptance. It is a concomitant of active experience. In my days as a skilled technician, I stood on the sidelines, directing the game and scoring. I was an observer and a manipulator of other people's experience. Now I join in the game. I win and I lose; I live and I learn.

This is the action of action research. It not only enhances the lives of the pupils. It empassions and enriches beyond all imaginings the personal lives of thinking practitioners. To Polanyi again (1958, p. 143): 'Having made a discovery, I shall never see the world again as before. My eyes have become different; I have made myself into a person seeing and thinking differently. I have crossed a gap, the heuristic gap which lies between problem and discovery.'

## Conclusion

Here is a way forward for teachers to gain, personally and professionally. There never has been such a need for the teaching profession to go public, either in a political sense, with appraisal, accountability, disputes about pay and conditions, all contributing to present the image of a profession afraid and weak; or in a moral sense, when we are poised on the brink of great sociological changes, such that the teaching profession could take a vigorous lead in determining the future of this country. Yet the greatest revolutions start with individuals, and this teaching revolution must start with individual teachers in their own classrooms who are attempting to make sense of their own practice.

# PART II

# PRACTICE

# Chapter 5

# How to Start an Action Research Study

## Introduction

This chapter, together with Chapter 6, 'Making sense of the data', offers ways of starting an action research study. These are not the only ways possible, but they are probably the most practical ones available at the moment. Chapters 7, 8 and 9 are case studies by three teachers, illustrating these techniques.

The chapter is divided into three parts: (1) Planning, (2) Practicalities, (3) Implications.

## 1 Planning

Educational reform begins with a sense of dissatisfaction with present practice. Six critical questions (Barrett and Whitehead, 1985) help teachers to set the scene ready for action:

1 What is your concern?
2 Why are you concerned?
3 What do you think you could do about it?
4 What kind of 'evidence' could you collect to help you make some judgement about what is happening?
5 How would you collect such 'evidence'?
6 How would you check that your judgement about what has happened is reasonably fair and accurate?

The answers will produce a practical assessment of the situation and a possible plan of attack. The action-reflection spiral is also brought into play:

1 I experience problems when some of my educational values are denied in practice.
2 I imagine a solution to those problems.
3 I act in the direction of the imagined solution.
4 I evaluate the outcome of the solution.
5 I modify my practice, plans and ideas in the light of the evaluation.

*An example to show the plans in practice*

In his work as a lecturer in the Department of Education at Bristol Polytechnic, Martin Forrest's concern was with both initial and in-service teacher education. He was also concerned to move forward his understanding of his own practice, and this led him to undertake his own research programme.

The following section is abstracted from his 1983 report 'The Teacher as Researcher – the use of historical artefacts in primary schools' which was his submission to the University of Bath in part fulfilment of the requirements for his MEd degree. All quotations are from this report.

Martin's approach 'followed the lines of an action research project aimed at improving the quality of learning in local primary schools, in which partnership between the external researcher and his school teacher associates (was) seen as of central importance'.

His project was, in fact, an example of action research working on two levels: his study of his own practice as an in-service supporter, and the studies of two teachers he encouraged in their investigations into their own classroom practices. The process and experience of action research applied equally to all those taking part.

Martin posed two sets of key questions at the outset of his study:

1 How can we know that an improvement has taken place in the school classroom? What criteria do we use to judge whether an innovation has led to an improvement in the quality of learning?
2 In the context of my work as an inservice tutor, how effective am I in my role as a disseminator and supporter of innovation? What evidence is there to support my claim to be helping teachers to improve the quality of their children's learning?

He decided to follow the action-reflection cycle (outlined on page 38) of

1 The statement of problems
2 The imagination of a solution

3 The implementation of a solution
4 The evaluation of the solution
5 The modification of practice in the light of the evaluation

He points out that this cycle operated at the two distinct but interrelated levels in his study: 'Firstly, the teacher researchers working in their own classrooms to improve the quality of their pupils' learning using historical artefacts, and secondly, this researcher himself seeking to disseminate, innovate and to support teacher researchers implementing this innovation in their schools.' The report is then organised to show the cycle in action for the two teachers, as well as the action of the researcher himself. Sections of the report focus on an evaluation of the implementation of the solutions by the two teachers, as well as an evaluation of his own involvement in this innovatory mode, together with suggestions for modification of his own practice in the light of this piece of research.

*1 Statement of problems*

Martin was dissatisfied with two aspects of his current practice: first, the assumption that the RD and D model was an acceptable research mode for the kind of curriculum development work in which he was engaged; and second, that although the Schools Council Project with which he had been associated (CSCP) had been one of the more successful of the projects which used the RD and D model, there was some evidence that this approach frequently led to a mismatch between the educational values of teachers using the materials and the values of the research team.

The criteria Martin identified as representative of his educational values were:

1 an attempt to present a selection of the BEST that has survived from ancient Greece and Rome and to make it available in the most readily communicated form to as many children as possible;
2 the EXCITEMENT of INVESTIGATING the ancient world;
3 what may be regarded as a 'democratic ideal' appropriate to a comprehensive school, an underlying assumption that here was a worthwhile experience for all pupils to enjoy, even if the pupils subsequently chose to reject it, rather than something reserved only for able linguists;
4 the researcher's faith in teachers to innovate and a belief in the capacity of teachers to assimilate new teaching approaches.

### 2 *Imagining a solution*

Martin hypothesised possible solutions to his main areas of concern.

First, in attempting to formulate a strategy that would involve himself and practitioners in a joint research endeavour, he referred to Avon's Working Paper on the School Curriculum (1982). This document refers to DES Circular 6/81 which emphasises the importance of partnership in curriculum planning.

His response to the problem of a mismatch in values was to begin by explaining value positions with his collaborators at the outset. The primary school teachers with whom he was to work were asked about their educational aims and to relate their work to official curriculum statements including the 'official' guidelines for using the materials.

Here was the potential for the teacher, equipped with cases of historical artefacts supplied by Bristol City Museum and some guidelines for their use, to operate against his/her own framework of values and with certain identified aims in mind. Martin, on the other hand, with his own set of values clearly identified, intended to make himself available to participating teachers as an encourager and sustainer of their own research activities. He hypothesised that by integrating these two solutions, he and the teachers would arrive at a way of teaching history that would match his educational values, which he spells out in recorded interviews (available for inspection).

### 3 *Implementing the solution*

The solution then led to two case studies of Avon primary school teachers with whom Martin had been working. Other primary school teachers were involved as well, but for his research purposes Martin focused on the two teachers. These two teachers had expressed a sense of dissatisfaction with their current practice, and so were particularly interested in trying out new approaches. They undertook to produce ongoing reports for their own school research, and to make these reports available for Martin's dissertation. He in turn undertook to make his dissertation available to them. Throughout, a reciprocal relationship was maintained.

He recounts:

> The first cycle of action-reflection in which Sue and Carol engaged with their children in association with the researcher is described in the two research reports which follow. In these reports an account is given of how the two teachers implemented

and evaluated their own solutions to the problems they experienced and how these processes were respectively monitored. The researcher's implementation is of his own solution to the problem of finding a demonstrably effective way of helping teachers to introduce innovation and to improve the quality of their pupils' education.

At the beginning of the project he established a core validation group including fourteen fellow students, and he presents a table of attendance at each of four meetings which shows that up to eleven people attended on any one occasion with a central core attending all the meetings.

The action research projects of the two teachers followed the same rigorous procedure as the overall project. The outline of one of the projects is given below.

*Sue Kilminster's project*

As criteria for her educational values, Sue was invited to consider the Aims of School Education (DES 1981)

1 to help pupils to develop lively, enquiring minds, the ability to question and argue rationally and to apply themselves to tasks and physical skills;
2 to help pupils acquire knowledge and skills relevant to adult life and employment in a fast-changing world;
3 to help pupils to use language and number effectively;
4 to instil respect for religious and moral values and tolerance of other races, religions and ways of life;
5 to help pupils to understand the world in which they live, and the interdependence of individuals, groups and nations;
6 to help pupils appreciate human achievements and aspirations.

Of these aims, she felt that aim 1 was of prime importance, but that the study of artefacts could also contribute to the development of moral values (aim 4). She also saw her work as contributing something to aims 2 and 6.

(a) STATEMENT OF PROBLEMS

Sue recognised the value of artefacts in providing a stimulus to learning not previously available to her which provided a contrast with a didactic/expository approach: 'I think something like . . . those sugar nippers caused so much interest – I think the shape is a very interesting one to the children – they begin to think of a grocery shop: who would go into a grocer's shop? . . . .' and she recognised the superiority of handling objects over photographs as a learning experience:

> If I'd, say, taken a photograph of those objects and said to the children 'Here's a photograph of these things, what do you really think about them?' I think within five minutes they'd have been really bored: 'Oh, it's a photograph.' Because they went around and tried to use them, suddenly it became realistic to them . . . a picture would have meant nothing.

However, there were several problems which arose from Sue's introduction of this innovation in her classroom. First, in regard to Sue's aim of helping her pupils to develop lively, enquiring minds, the ability to question and argue rationally – Sue was concerned to involve all children in the discussion and to help them to produce rational argument leading to tentative identification of the nature, purpose and age of the objects themselves. The guidelines for handling objects (Avon LEA, 1982) refer to opportunities for the children to 'talk and listen to each other; – to think, argue and make rational deduction.'

Here she recognised the need to provide an air of mystery which would enhance the group discussion and the process of deduction. Together, she and Martin adopted the suggestion of first, wrapping the objects, and later of introducing a 'feely box' in which the children needed to grope around and guess what the objects inside were. This then led to:

(b) IMAGINING SOLUTIONS

The plan put forward by Sue was that each group of 4/5 children should have one object to study. To begin with the object would be presented for them to feel 'blind', thus encouraging from the outset a fair degree of speculation as to what the object might be made of, what shape it felt like, how heavy it was and so on. In due course they would be able to see the object as well as feel it and thence be encouraged to talk through as a group (along the lines of the guide) the nature of the object, what it might be made of, how it might be made, what it might have been used for and what kind of person might have used it.

Each group in turn was to discuss their object in front of the video camera while the rest of the children proceeded with other set work, the intention being to record as fully as possible the children's reaction to the objects and the group discussion as it developed.

Second, in regard to the back-up resources, Sue's idea was that after the initial study of the object and after tentative conclusions had been reached about its nature and purpose, each group should attempt to relate their object to an historical context; there would then be an opportunity for each group to work on a series of mini-investigations to develop their ideas using art/craft and written work and to report back to the whole class in due course.

Third, Sue planned to help the children relate all six objects to a time-line and to display all the work generated by the children in such a way that all children might benefit from the shared experience.

(c) IMPLEMENTING THE SOLUTIONS

A video camera recorded the early events as each group studied its object for the first time. Videorecordings were presented to the validation panel meetings as follows:

THREE GROUPS STUDY THEIR OBJECT WRAPPED IN PAPER.
THREE GROUPS STUDY THEIR OBJECT USING A FEELY BOX.

In the event the feely box was a plain cardboard box with a hole cut in it for one small arm to be inserted and with the lid firmly closed. Altogether two one-hour sessions were devoted to this activity, with each group being recorded at work in turn. Sue kept control of the operations by ensuring that each member of the group had an opportunity of handling the object and of contributing to the discussion. She also ensured that the key questions were asked by each group. Sue avoided telling the children what their object might be until the very end of the group discussion, though she did help them to arrive at a conclusion if there were any difficulties (for example, a lemon squeezer), in this case drawing upon a contribution from a boy in another group.

Back-up resources were supplied by Martin. Each group was asked to find out about their object in relation to the period from which it came. In this way, Sue hoped to help the children to relate this object to its social/cultural context.

After spending three weeks following up their object, they finally displayed their work. Each group then talked to the rest of the class about their findings and questions came thick and fast from their classmates.

(d) EVALUATING THE SOLUTION

First, there was clear evidence of the groups undertaking a more sustained discussion second time round.

> *Sue*: I think, speaking generally, to begin with, all of them looked at the objects much more closely this time. Instead of saying: 'Oh, yes, this is it. I'm not sure what it's made from, it's made from this, made from that,' I think all of them looked at the objects more closely . . .

The children generally showed increased confidence in their approach to the objects and were willing to speculate freely without fear of getting the wrong answer. Sometimes several possibilities were discussed.

> *Sue*: I think they were all, when they looked at the objects first of all, a bit worried they might get it wrong. This time they realised it didn't really matter and they could all guess differently.

The feely box also helped to sustain discussion; the children were encouraged to speculate about the objects by touch in the first instance. After playing back the videotape, Sue felt that the feely box was the best way of introducing the objects.

There is some evidence that the children actually concentrated more on the process of handling the objects in the early stages because of the presence of the videocamera. The point was made at the second validation meeting that this need not be seen as a drawback but as a positive AID to the process of improvement.

The validation group viewed the videorecording that refers to this phase:

CHILDREN'S WORK AND VTR OF CHILDREN TALKING TO THE REST OF THE CLASS ABOUT THEIR WORK

Arising from the class study of these objects, three children went on trips with their parents and brought back information which was related to the objects.

> *General comment by Sue*: I was amazed at the quality of the questions being asked by the children (of the groups giving the talk) because they were actually thinking about the time of the object and asking questions about that time.

(e) MODIFICATION OF PRACTICE

The report presented to the validation group represented one completed cycle of action/reflection by Sue and had incorporated within it a number of suggestions for modification of her practice. One of the points discussed relates to seeing how far the children can work systematically on their own.

In the course of the third validation group meeting, Sue indicated that, as a result of seeing the videotape of Carol Smith's five and six year olds and the extent to which they had learnt to work independently of the teacher, she would like to see how far her eight and nine year olds had now developed the ability to work autonomously as the result of the work she had been doing. 'I would like to use the experience and just give them the objects without any help at all.' Accordingly, Sue planned two weeks after the final validation group meeting for Martin to videorecord the whole class, divided this time into new groups, each working with a completely new object. Sue had thus embarked on a new cycle, spurred on by her colleagues from another school and taking into account the points which arose from her evaluation of the earlier implementation of work with artefacts.

REPORT ON THE VALIDATION GROUP MEETINGS

From the outset, the validation group members were presented with the two sets of questions posed on page 58. Both sets of questions were concerned with providing criteria for judging improvement and with trying to identify evidence of improvement of a kind which would satisfy the validation group.

At all meetings the validation group looked at the research project operating on its two levels. They considered Martin's overall project as well as those of the two teachers. In all instances, the group identified what its members considered to be criteria that indicated an improvement in education, and instances in action that fulfilled those criteria.

It was agreed that evidence should be collected in the form of audio and videotape recordings of Martin's involvement and, where appropriate, examples of children's work with a view to demonstrating improvement taking place over a period of two to three months. (Mention has already been made of videorecordings available.)

Following the first validation group meeting, Martin discussed with the two teachers how the action research might be given a sharper focus, bearing in mind that the intention was not for the researchers to engage in a traditional form of educational research activity, but to monitor improvements taking place over time in relation to the teacher's own educational values and to look at particular children in the class for particular improvements taking place.

The reports show this systematic identification of criteria and instances of those criteria in action. They also include documentary evidence from the recorded discussions of the validation groups to show agreement about the criteria and that improvement had taken place.

> The thing that impressed me most was the way, somehow, these children came to their conclusions through dialogue and discussion themselves.
>
> I just wanted to say I was very impressed by the evidence of lively enquiring minds.
>
> 'It couldn't be a library book, because you couldn't keep a book out of a library as long as that'. Obviously they've got some concept of time, haven't they?

During all the validation group meetings, Martin was questioned closely about his role, and required to produce documentary evidence that he had moved forward his own practice, through helping the teachers to develop a deeper understanding of their practices.

4 *Evaluating the solution and proposals for modification of practice in the light of the evaluation*

The evaluation of the solution reviews Martin's educational values, the denial of which inspired him to engage in the research study.

In the final validation group meetings, Carol, questioned closely by members of the validation group, identified Martin's enthusiasm as an important factor in the dialogue which took place between them over four months.

> *Jack*: You talked about Martin being enthusiastic. How would you describe that enthusiasm, looking back over time?
> *Carol*: Well, he's got faith in what he's doing . . .

Martin's evaluation has led him to want to widen the scope of his studies. He continues to be involved in helping other colleagues with their own action research projects.

The foregoing is an outline of a classic action research study. Copyright for the report rests with Martin Forrest who may be approached for further information. His address is on page 151.

## 2 Practicalities

This section aims to point out a common-sense procedure for starting an action research study.

1 Start small. Even though the project itself may not be small (for example, introducing a staff appraisal scheme; seeking to enhance the quality of oracy throughout the school), the study itself should focus in the initial stages on aspects rather than the whole. Action research is strategic, and planning the strategies is very important. So, for example, if the study is to do with staff-appraisal schemes, start perhaps with gathering opinion on the state of the art, or if staff want to remain anonymous or identified in answering questionnaires, or how the staff themselves would set about the task. If the study is to do with improving oracy, focus on one or two groups to see how to improve their problems. Action research is sequential and cumulative. Each step will act as a springboard to the next. The insights gained enhance people's willingness to participate; they lead to establishing an atmosphere of genuine enquiry. It is a false economy to leap into a large project, ready to tackle each and every aspect of the situation. Small, considered steps are more thrifty of people's time, energy and motivation.

2 Plan carefully. This does not involve the setting of predetermined objectives; for example, it is my objective to have covered chapters 1–3 by Christmas; to have identified all the problems in the first-year science curriculum by half term. It is the experience of many teachers that such objectives will be discarded very shortly after the project begins. There is often a wide gap between what we think will happen and what actually does happen. Shortly after they begin, many teachers find that specific problems are symptoms of much more generalised underlying problems of practice and attitudes.

It is important, however, to plan how an action research study is to be set up: which problem areas are to be tackled first; which classes/ colleagues are to be intimately involved; who needs to be consulted and kept informed; what machinery exists or must be set up to allow for feedback and free exchange of views; what resources may be needed – for example, tape or video recorders/ancillary help. Time invested in planning pays high dividends. An unplanned study which starts with a bang but then sputters around a bit may well turn out to be a damp squib – unreliable and potentially dangerous.

3 Set a realistic time-scale. It is necessary in the planning stages to set time-scales, but they must be realistic enough to cope with the unpredictability of human beings and the circumstances they find themselves in. It is perhaps wisest to set two time limits; first an ideal, recognising that ideals are what we strive to achieve but possibly never quite achieve, and a second of a more generous nature, although you must stress that times must be adhered to in order to maintain the credibility of the project in the eyes of colleagues. Any one-year enquiry that takes three is bound to raise a few eyebrows, unless it is spelt out in public that the original study brought into focus other, originally unrecognised, issues that deserved penetrating study. It is inherent in the action-reflection cycle that this frequently occurs. Any project that uncovers other issues and then proceeds to deal with them systematically must be very public about what it is doing; and point out in turn the time-scales to be expected in the new cycles of enquiry.

4 Involve others. Action research is for independents, but not for solitaries. Solitary action loses its claim to research, for an isolated study cannot be held up to the public scrutiny and validation procedures that qualify it as research.

Action research requires that other people will be involved. In most research studies, but not all, other people are involved as participants of the research and as validators of its findings. Action research is research WITH rather than ON other people.

Involvement of people will operate at some or all of the following levels in any one enquiry:

- Participants in an action research study. Mrs Smith will explain carefully how she hopes to improve the educational situation HERE AND NOW. Participants will probably be the children and other colleagues.
- Colleagues as participants. Mrs Smith will enlist the support of the rest of her department, her professional tutor, her deputy head, her headteacher, her adviser – anyone whose support is appropriate.
- Colleagues as observers. She will be at pains to let the rest of the staff know what she is doing. She will aim to de-mystify her study, making it public and accessible.
- Colleagues/participants as validators. She will plan at the begin-

ning to have a special validation group of about three to eight colleagues who will criticise her work, challenge her findings, and agree with her criteria in support of her claim to know that she has improved her educational situation. The main participants in the enquiry (for example, children or colleagues) may also act as validators, agreeing that Mrs Smith's claims are valid; that they (for example, the children) really have moved in the direction that she claims.

Readers of study findings. The readers may be other colleagues, advisers, university tutors, the public – anyone who is interested enough to read the reports of the studies. People from all walks of educational action research life are encouraged to produce and publish their work, with a view to entering into correspondence with interested parties (see, for example, Case Studies; CARN bulletins, pp. 146). Until recently, publication seemed to be reserved for the academics, and journals tended to be strictly learned. There is a movement towards scholarly but common-sense pieces, free of jargon, and accessible to ordinary teachers in ordinary schools.

5 Keep others informed. Even if people are not directly involved in the project, they should be kept informed of what is going on. Unidentified activities quickly assume an aura of mystique, or, worse, furtiveness, as if some subversive activity were being conducted. Any action research study should be announced to as wide a clientele as possible. For example, if Mr Jones is about to start his study he should inform colleagues in his academic or pastoral department, his deputy head/professional tutor, any administrative organisers whose professional life touches his, his headteacher, and, if possible, let the whole staff know by an announcement in the staff meeting or a memo on the notice board. This may sound like blowing one's own trumpet quite loudly, but publicity soon tones down and the message will have been conveyed. If Mr Jones is conducting a study on his practice which involves the children, it is a good idea to let parents know and, as Zita Gisborne did (page 103), invite them along to a special meeting.

6 Arrange for feedback. This is part of the good management of teaching, and particularly so of an action research project. It is important to let others know any results as soon as possible after the event. So, for example, if a validation meeting has taken place, and the conversation has been tape recorded, it is important to get the transcripts to the participants quickly. (Transcribing is a lengthy

business, and the difficulties are often underestimated. It takes seven to ten times as long to transcribe an account as to record it. On that basis, a ten-minute recording will take an hour to transcribe; an hour's recording will take seven to ten hours. Some time spent in the transcribing is inevitably wasted in understanding what is said, and in deciding what actually to transcribe. What is the message amidst the false starts and changed directions? How many of the asides should be included? How much is relevant? Then, having decided what is to be written down, the transcriber has to type it up. For teachers who have no secretarial help, typing can be very time consuming. The advice to researchers who use audio or videotape recording as a database is to keep the recording as short and to the point as possible. Set a reasonable time for transcription, and stick to the deadline.)

Regular reports, either verbal or written, are necessary. If possible, set a schedule for getting reports out – every half term, say. Such a schedule will also keep the researcher up to date. It is inevitable that such reports will not be read by as many people as hoped; but again the deed has been done. Action research is a political process, and anticipation is necessary to avoid friction.

Feedback is a necessary part of the action research process. It acts as a corrective device, or can give new directions to the project. If people see that their opinions are catered for and valued, they will participate gladly, make constructive rather than destructive comments, and seek personally to move the whole project forward. When arranging for feedback, it is important to build into the machinery the publication of the feedback and its resultant action. For if people take the step of expressing their opinions, this is a personal commitment, which must then be publicly recorded and honoured.

7 Organise a writing schedule. Right from the start, time should be set aside for writing up, formally or informally.

Writing in itself is a tool for thought. A number of researchers (see, for example, Hustler *et al.*, 1986; Walker, 1985) find that the act of writing clarifies ideas. The working out of a sentence gets rid of confusion, and the discipline of having to organise the subject matter on paper helps to organise it in the mind (see, for example, Rowland's *The Enquiring Classroom* (1984)).

Writing up is essential for an action research study. It is characteristic that the study will change direction, or that the researcher will change direction, or that circumstances will force things on to a new tack. It is inevitable that the identification of problems will reveal new problems, and that as each solution is tested, accepted or rejected, so new alternatives will arise for consideration. This is the basis of such an approach, that it has the flexibility built in to allow for creativity and spontaneity.

Rather than being viewed as a complete journey from start to finish, action research should be seen as a series of short hops. It is important to capture the action of the interludes. Once a section has gone its impact has gone as well, and seen in retrospect it will certainly appear different than it was at the time. We tend to interpret the past against our experience of the present. Immediate recording of events as they happen will avoid inevitable skewing of the data, and give a truer picture of the action and how we interpreted the action.

## 3 Implications

Be prepared for some or all of thc following.

### (1) *Thinking will change*

Often, teachers embarking on an action research study have set expectations of what is going to happen, and then very quickly have to alter their whole concept. Typical comments from colleages include:

*Brian*: Three days into the project I had to throw all my thinking out of the window. It just did not turn out as I expected.

*Fiona*: No, we hadn't planned on that happening, but it's much better that way.

*Peter* (of his staff): It's nice to see them have the confidence to decide collectively to abandon that road and start all over again.

### (2) *Mistakes will happen*

It is important to realise from the start that things might not run smoothly and to arrange the necessary armoury in advance. School life is often unpredictable and so are people. For all sorts of reasons, things might go wrong in the enquiry: equipment will not be there when needed; timetables are suddenly changed; people are absent; the researcher has a splitting headache on the day of filming; reports are not ready for the staff meeting; and so on. The three case studies at the heart of this book describe such difficulties in detail. They also describe how their authors encountered problems and attempted to rise above them.

These potential difficulties emphasise the 'people-centredness' of action research. An enquiry is dependent on a dialogue between persons for its success. Critics see this as one of its limitations, pointing out that a research design that is so heavily focused on human factors will founder in the vagaries of human error, and this point is well justified. Supporters of action research see this dependency as a strength, stressing the need for a one-to-one understanding between persons as an ideologically appropriate way to approach human enquiries.

Tolerance and good humour are vital. The action researcher is in a position of leadership, and in the public eye. If he can keep his head he will quickly earn a reputation for himself and his project that they are of worth. Respect is won dearly, and it is earned not by vaunting success but by coping with potential failure.

### *(3) Politics will intrude*

Action research is political, in that it is to do with change. Often an individual researcher will find himself at odds with the established system. He might want to experiment with a new style of desk arrangement to encourage active participation. The noise generated in the initial stages of the children moving the desks could well attract frowns from other colleagues (there is a need for advance information here to warn colleagues that something new is afoot); the frowns and staffroom comments may well chill his enthusiasm to have another go. Or an investigation into the use of resources may unearth data about their allocation, and persons who have benefited will want to discourage further research. Or the success of an enquiry into alternative teaching styles may well bring pressure from the Head on other colleagues to try out new styles for themselves, and lead to unpopularity of the original scheme. These examples are not invented; they are the experiences of real practitioners who suffered at the hands of others because of their insistence on moving nearer to discovering their own truth.

This is a cautionary note: that opposition will come the way of the action researcher who goes public. People are usually afraid of change and will often resist it by whatever means they have available. Action research needs teachers of courage.

# Chapter 6
# Making Sense of the Data

## Introduction

An action research enquiry needs systematic planning and application, and this orderly procedure often seems unattainable within an already over-crowded day. Even when the study is formally under way, teachers will find themselves overwhelmed by the sheer volume of the data, with so many aspects as possible contenders for detailed attention. It is very difficult, but very important, to try to make consistent sense of what is going on. This chapter gives guidelines. It is essentially a practical chapter, with 'how to do' advice, how to make sense of a potentially confusing field.

The contents follow an action-reflection spiral of identifying a problem; imagining a solution; implementing the solution; observing the effects; evaluating the outcomes; modifying actions and ideas in the light of the evaluation; re-planning for the next action step. It is easier to make sense of things, including data, if this type of organised action-reflection plan is adopted.

1 Which problem? How to identify and focus on specific problem areas.
2 Collecting the data: the options for different methods. Which method for which purpose?
3 Monitoring the action. How to observe efficiently and effectively.
4 Analysing the data. How does a teacher make sense of it all? What does it actually mean?
5 Synthesising the data. Organising and presenting the data to the public.

## 1 Which problem?

It is sometimes very difficult to identify a specific problem. Most curriculum and personal practice reform begins with a sense of dissatisfaction: 'There is something wrong here, but I can't quite put my finger on it.' Sometimes the problems are explicit: 'I am not succeeding because my out-dated machinery is still Imperial; I need metric', and this is a definite need for resources. How to get the resources is another question and may need an action-reflection campaign! Usually questions to do with educational reform are questions of value, and usually those values are being denied in practice. 'I want X to happen, but Y always seems to happen. How can I change the situation to be X rather than Y?'

In his *Action research planner* (1982) Kemmis starts the action with a general plan:

> You do not have to begin with a 'problem'. All you need is a general idea that something might be improved. Your general idea may stem from a promising new idea of the recognition that existing practice falls short of aspirations. In either case you must centre attention on
>
> - What is happening now?
> - In what sense is this problematic?
> - What can I do about it?
>
> General starting points will look like –
>
> - I would like to improve the . . .
> - Some people are unhappy about . . .
>   What can I do to change the situation?
> - I am perplexed by . . .
> - . . . is a source of irritation. What can I do about it?
> - I have an idea I would like to try out in my class.
> - How can the experience of . . . be applied to . . .?
> - Just what do I do with respect to . . .?

The case studies in this book, detailed or glossed in reporting, all indicate a dissatisfaction with present practice and a desire to change it.

Kemmis sensibly advises:

> Avoid issues which you can do nothing about. Questions like the relationship between socio-economic status and achievement, between ability and tendency to ask questions in class may be interesting, but they have tenuous links with action. Stick with

issues in which you do something which has potential for improvement. Remember that strategic action is your way to improve practice and your understanding of apparent and real constraints on change.

It is always helpful to be aware of the limitations of innovations before embracing them as potential answers to each and every problem. Action research is not always the answer. As a general rule it may be said that action research is appropriate to educational questions of value, where the desire is to improve the situation through an understanding of personal practice. It is not always appropriate for problem areas where personal practice is not the issue. On page 4 there is a point about the 'macro-micro' issue. Action research is usually applicable to 'micro' areas of personal practice, but not often to the 'macro' areas of socio-economic situations.

Examples of issues where action research would be suitable:

- I would like to improve the quality of oracy in my English lessons.
- I would like to introduce computer-based learning into Humanities. How can I evaluate its impact/desirability?
- Why the decline in the popularity of cross-country?
- How can I persuade the staff not to smoke in school? Am I justified in wanting to do so?
- Communication in staff policy meetings seems to be one-way. How can I encourage a freer exchange of ideas?

Examples of issues where action research would not be suitable:

- What is the link between children's socio-economic status and their enjoyment of literature?
- What is the number of children in school from single-parent families?
- What is the relationship between single-parent families and school attendance?
- How does teaching style relate to pupil progress?

Having mapped out the general area of concern, try now to focus more specifically on something you feel you can do something about. Talk it over with at least one other critical friend. Jot down ideas. Writing ideas down is often far more cost-productive than gazing out of the window; writing sharpens the wit and focuses the attention. And there is something to be seen for your efforts, which is pleasing in itself.

Keep the issues within manageable proportions; keep them relevant to yourself and the people in your care. Do not be concerned at this stage with other people's problems. Sort out your own first.

Kemmis advises:

> . . . In choosing the area in which you prefer to work you must attend to the following criteria:
> - How important is the issue to you
> - How important it is for your students
> - What opportunities there are to explore the area
> - Who might be interested in helping
> - The manageability of the task
>
> Remember that radical transformations are not easily achieved: be prepared to be sustained by modest success.
>
> Settle on an idea YOU can do something about.

## 2 Collecting the data

There are two different, though related, perspectives to this question:
(i) which techniques are available for classroom data collection
(ii) which techniques are appropriate for which reason.

There is a comprehensive survey of data collection methods in Walker (1985) *Doing research* and in Hopkins (1985) *A teacher's guide to classroom research.* Both texts outline the various traditional methods: field notes, audio tape recording, pupil diaries, interviews and discussions, video tape recording, questionnaires, sociometry, documentary evidence, slide/tape photography, case study. Hopkins's Chapter 6 presents a taxonomy of these classroom research techniques pointing out the advantages and disadvantages of each one (see Fig. 6.1).

This present book is not primarily a 'methodological' text, and the treatment given to data collection methods is cursory. What follows is a brief survey.

Data collection techniques fall into three broad categories:

### *(a) Paper and pen methods*

PERSONAL FIELD NOTES

The teacher systematically keeps notes of the class situation, either while the lesson is in progress or immediately afterwards. This is more than keeping a record book as a kind of diary which will record

| Technique | Advantage(s) | Disadvantage(s) | Use(s) |
|---|---|---|---|
| Field Notes | simple; on going; personal; aide memoire | subjective; needs practice | • specific issue<br>• case study<br>• general impression |
| Audio Tape Recording | versatile; accurate; provides ample data | transcription difficult; time consuming; often inhibiting | • detailed evidence<br>• diagnostic |
| Pupil Diaries | provides pupils perspective | subjective | • diagnostic<br>• triangulation |
| Interviews and Discussions | can be teacher–pupil, observer–pupil, pupil–pupil | time consuming | • specific in depth information |
| Video Tape Recorder | visual and comprehensive | awkward and expensive; can be distracting | • visual material<br>• diagnostic |
| Questionnaires | highly specific; easy to administer; comparative | time consuming to analyse; problem of 'right' answers | • specific information & feedback |
| Sociometry | easy to administer; provides guide to action | can threaten isolated pupils | • analyses social relationships |
| Documentary evidence | illuminative | difficult to obtain; time consuming | • provides context & information |
| Slide/Tape Photography | illuminative; promotes discussion | difficult to obtain; superficial | • illustrates critical incidents |
| Case Study | accurate; representative; uses range of techniques | time consuming | • comprehensive overview of an issue<br>• publishable format |

*Fig. 6.1. Taxonomy of classroom research techniques*

only ground covered and materials used. It will document significant aspects of the action: for example, two normally uncommunicative children responded to others today; I tried a new seating arrangement. Such notes can feature strongly in the validation phases (see Chapter 11) when the enquiry and its strategies may be made public and available to other colleagues for criticism, challenge and, it is hoped, approbation.

PUPILS' DIARIES

These can provide direct feedback from the pupils' perspective. Pupils are required to keep notebooks or files on their responses to their lessons. Guidance may be given by the teacher as to points to consider, but there should be little constraint on the pupils as to what they should write. The fear of censorship will remove some spontaneity, and if one of the reasons for diaries is to gauge the situation honestly from the pupils' point of view, they should be encouraged to respond openly and honestly without fear of reprisal. If the teacher has the child's permission to read the diary and comment, a valuable dialogue may be set up.

Again, such diaries are very useful resources in the validation phases, but if the diaries have been kept on a confidential basis, the pupils' permission must always be sought prior to any form of publication.

QUESTIONNAIRES

These are notoriously difficult to create in order to get the information desired, and they are liable to misuse. The section in Hopkins (1985) is excellent on this point.

In an action research enquiry, questionnaires will probably be used in an exploratory fashion to get an idea of trends. Enquiries conducted in an action research mode are usually to do with values, and it is very difficult to capture the nuances of opinion associated with questions of value through the precise formulation of questionnaires. Questions of value often take the form of 'Yes, but . . .', and this sort of tentativeness is not accommodated in questionnaires.

*(b) 'Live' methods*

SOCIOMETRIC METHODS

These are useful in analysing social relationships, but threatening to pupils if not sensitively administered. In such approaches pupils are invited to record in some way their attractions and aversions to others. So, for example, they could write down the name of the child they would best (or least) like to work with, sit next to, be appointed as monitor with, and so on. The teacher can then make an analysis of the information for her own uses in attempting to enhance the social and emotional climate of the classroom. In Fig. 6.2 C is in trouble, while B is favoured.

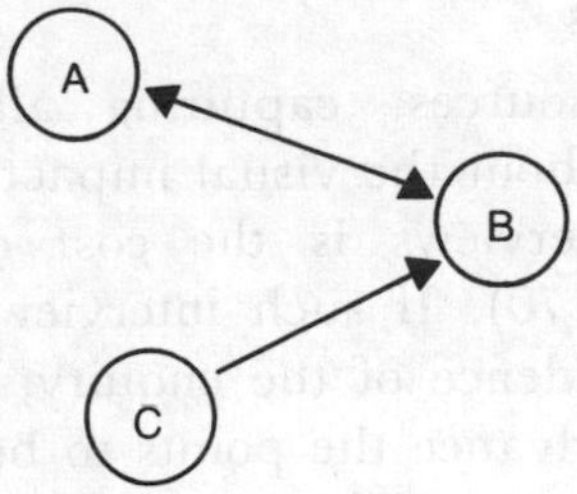


*Fig. 6.2.*

The work of Leslie Button is invaluable in this area, particularly his *Developmental group work with adolescents* (1974), and his practical workbooks, *Group tutoring for the form teacher* (1981, 1982). Also valuable is the work of Baldwin and Wells (1979–81) and McGuire and Priestley (for example, 1981). For a comprehensive bibliography of work in this area see McNiff (1986).

INTERVIEWS AND DISCUSSIONS

These are extremely valuable sources of data, but very time consuming. Care must be taken to limit the number of people present to about seven, if the idea is for everyone to contribute. Larger groups might inhibit the less forward members. The information from such gatherings is not easily retrieved unless it is recorded which has its own inherent difficulties (see 'Ostensive methods' below). Live interviews are, however, very valuable in giving immediate feedback on the enquiry and suggestions for its future. In this way such conversations are crucial in the validation of the researcher's claims that an improvement has taken place.

### (c) *Ostensive methods*

SLIDE/TAPE PRESENTATIONS

These are difficult to obtain and limited in what they portray. The use of a camera in class can be very intrusive, even more so than a videorecorder which, once *in situ*, becomes part of the furniture after the first flush of interest from the children has died away. Photographs portray 'stills' of the action, and it is most difficult to obtain just those moments that are significant instances. Such presentations are valuable, however, in the publication of data in an abstracted form, that is as a summary of the enquiry, pointing to other ways in which the data is presented in a more synthesised form.

AUDIOTAPED INTERVIEWS

These are valuable sources, capturing all the nuances of real conversation, albeit without the visual impact. A real deterrent in the use of audiotaped interviews is the cost of time and energy in transcribing (see page 70). If such interviews are to be used as an integral part of the evidence of the enquiry, it is in the researcher's interests to decide in advance the points to be covered. A ten minute interview will take at least an hour to transcribe.

VIDEOTAPING THE ACTION

This is the nearest to encapsulated reality that modern classroom technology allows at present. Obvious disadvantages are the cost or availability of the equipment; training of personnel in its use; intrusiveness of the equipment and operator; transcribing the conversation. Such difficulties are not insurmountable. Pupils may be taught to be efficient operators, enjoying the task and feeling a responsible part of the action. The intrusiveness is overcome if the equipment is a regular feature of normal practice. Availability and questions of resources is another matter, to do with the support of teachers (see Chapter 12).

### *Attitudes towards data collection*

It is important to be aware of attitudes towards data collection as well as the variety of techniques available. The techniques described are all useful in their own way. It is difficult, when first starting out on an enquiry, to determine which method is going to be most suitable for which purpose. The following guidelines are problem-orientated:

- Is the problem in my practice technical in nature? Can it be solved, for example, by a direct appeal to administration for an input of resources?

*Examples*:

- I need more textbooks
- There are too many pupils in my group for my individual approach
- The blinds in my room are ineffective for adequate blackout

- Is the problem in my practice closed in nature? Can it be solved, for example, by a direct appeal to observation of the situation? If so, I may use techniques that will give me quick impressions such as questionnaires, field notes, photography.

*Examples*:

- Some children in my group seem left out of the total action. Is the geography of the classroom wrong?
- Information about resources seems not to be reaching everyone in the department. Are they aware of information channels?
- Some students seem never to get their homework in on time. Does this mean more specific guidance from me in organisation of study timetables?

• Is the problem in my practice open-ended in nature? Is it a question of values? If so, I probably need a more comprehensive medium for gathering the data and getting an overall picture, such as audiotaped discussions, videotaped lessons, interviews with groups and other colleagues.

*Examples*:

- Why is a particular group in my geography class hostile to the subject and to me?
- Why is there such a high truancy rate on Friday afternoons?
- How can I encourage more pupil participation in my English lessons?

There are, of course logistical criteria to be borne in mind as well as the evaluative ones already mentioned, such as amount of time available, cost of medium, number of people involved, and so on.

The business of data collection is usually eclectic, that is using every and any techniquc as seems appropriate to the task. Things tend to fall into place as the study goes on, and it is easy to learn which technique seems most appropriate to which situation. It is also true that teachers develop personal leanings towards certain techniques, as well as antipathies; videorecorders, for example, seem wonderful machines until they go wrong in class (often operator error). It is essential to keep this sort of setback in perspective and to develop a sense of balance.

## 3 Which data?

A common and worrying problem for teacher–researchers is that they often gather so much data that they rapidly become overwhelmed by it all. Is it all necessary? Is it all relevant? How does one make sense of the flood of data that pours in?

The situation is doubly confusing when the main focus of the original study seems to get lost in the mountain of information. For example, Jill, head of department, started her study into monitoring pupils' achievement in Home Economics. She started examining the style of tests that were in common use, usually summative, and decided to try some sort of formative assessment. In so doing, she discovered that the type of assessment determined style of teaching, and she was forced to break off from the original study concerning testing procedures to investigate what she and other colleagues were doing in their everyday teaching. The whole focus seemed to swing from assessment to teaching style. As the study progressed they decided that both teaching style and method of assessment were interdependent, and that the process was cyclical in nature rather than linear, and her study caused her to examine the whole curriculum for the department. In the intermediate stages of coming to this realisation, the original idea seemed to get lost. During the study the amounts of data from her own classes and those of colleagues, as well as of departmental meetings and discussions with colleagues, became monumental, and Jill became anxious about the whole business. The project at one time was in jeopardy of being overtaken by the need to record the data, and much ground was lost from paying too much attention to the detail rather than the overall picture.

In an action research study it is important to keep things in perspective and to remember that plans may well change as other issues are unearthed. Certainly the perspective may well alter. What started for me as an evaluation of my teaching in personal and social education in 1981 has turned into a major study of educating for personhood in 1987, with every likelihood that the research field will widen further.

It is useful, in deciding which data are relevant, to try to identify and home in on the focal points of the enquiry. Parlett and Hamilton (1972) (page 15) call this 'progressive focusing', that is, as the enquiry proceeds, so key issues become relevant. Subsidiary, irrelevant data is shelved (though never destroyed) and attention is focused on what is central.

Care should be taken to store all the data until the time of the formal study is over. Certain issues may be latent and come to the fore only with the passage of time. For example, Peter had a wealth of tape-recorded conversations with his pupils covering some three years of lessons. His main focus was to encourage oracy in his pupils. He could successfully point to an improvement in their oral competencies over the years. In the third year of his study, however, he shifted the focus of his enquiry, hypothesising that his own teaching style, whether sympathetic or autocratic, influenced the degree of oral competence in the children. He thought he could note a change in types of words used by the children, depending on their degree of assurance and intimacy. It seemed that the more 'humane' his lessons became, the more there was an emphasis on 'being' words rather than 'having' words, much in accordance with the ideas of Erich Fromm (for example, 1978). He could go back to his carefully stored tapes and carry out a detailed analysis of the emphasis in vocabulary and quality of language that seemed to develop in the children.

The question of which data is initially difficult to resolve, but time does seem to sort it out.

## 4 Monitoring the data

Keeping track of events is sometimes difficult, but essential if the study is to be systematic and legitimate when it comes to public attention. The methods of monitoring would be much the same as those recorded in the previous section on 'Which data?', but the personnel may well vary in monitoring. This may be done by the teacher–researcher, by a colleague or group of colleagues, or by the students themselves.

Key issues to do with different styles of monitoring include the following:

*Self-monitoring*

Keep a diary. It need only take about ten minutes to record what you have done at the end of each stage of your work, along with a few ideas about success and difficulties. Be rigorous about this; make it a habit; and if you slip on occasion, pick up the action again as quickly as possible and keep the diary going.

Write up accounts regularly. Set yourself some sort of easy schedule, every two, three or four weeks. Anything longer than four weeks will probably result in forgotten items. Share your accounts with a critical group.

Check back frequently to the original issue. Are you sticking to the point, or has the enquiry changed its focus? Be careful to record any such shift in emphasis, as this will possibly be the basis for future aspects of the enquiry.

*Colleague(s) monitoring*

In the initial stages of the enquiry it is essential to attract people who are going to be sympathetic to what you are trying to do. Their understanding will be significant in enabling you to develop an understanding of your own practice without feeling threatened by hostile elements. There will be enough critical reaction later when you come to present your enquiry in the public arena. At the same time, colleagues must be able to criticise supportively, in order to move your own ideas forward.

Arrange for regular, scheduled meetings with the colleague(s). It is important to get regular feedback on how the project is going. More will be said about this in Chapter 11, dealing with validation procedures.

*Students monitoring*

It is sometimes possible for students to have a quite different view of events and reactions than their teacher–researcher. Feedback from students can be revealing, not only of their own feelings, but of how they think the teacher is getting on. There is often a gap between the two sets of perceptions. Students can be the most critical, and also the most rewarding of monitors, and, although it takes courage to involve them in interpretations of teacher actions, such involvement can prove very heartening and stimulating.

*Joint monitoring*

Elliott and Adelman (1973) (see page 15) suggested triangulation as being potentially powerful in getting to the heart of the matter in pooling information and perceptions. 'Triangulation' is commonly used to refer to the process of obtaining information on a subject from three or more independent sources.

More generally, meetings of teachers, students and observers who join together in mutual interpretations of events are most valuable. The procedure is made even more dynamic if the meeting is audio- or videotaped, and the results then submitted to critical assessment by another validation group (see Chapter 11).

All of these methods and personnel are available, and it is up to the individual teacher–researcher to choose the medium he feels is the most appropriate to his study and its publication.

## 5 Analysing the data

The philosophy of action research suggests that an appropriate form of analysis would be through discussion of criteria and areas of concern as well as isolated instances of behaviour. Analysis is to do with making sense of what is going on in real life. Itemised instances will give indications only of how frequently people do things rather than why they do them. Such a notion sticks at observational or descriptive levels. In order to be explanatory, analysis has to look at the total action in order to suggest how one aspect will influence another.

Making sense means deciding on what could be termed 'sense' in the first place, explaining why this rather than other actions are termed 'sense', and suggesting how the educative action in question approximates to the sense. If a group considers the action in class as seen live or on video, for example, they can agree criteria that will epitomise the sense they are trying to establish. The study begins with the idea of improving areas of practice. The validation group will then agree instances of action that show an improvement of practice, that is identify criteria that will indicate this improvement and agree instances to show those criteria in action. They can attempt to make sense of the data by trying to explain what is going on within a real situation, rather than obtain information of a statistical nature about how often categories of actions are happening (which is how much 'traditional' analysis is conducted).

## 6 Synthesising the data

Synthesising the data means putting it all together in such a form that it may be easily communicated to, and comprehended by, other people. Analysis of an action research study implies identifying and agreeing criteria in action which can be used to explain what has happened or to indicate that improvement has taken place. Synthesis is how to explain the action in order to maintain it. This point is taken up in Chapters 12 and 13, but briefly here the points at issue are:

– the need for collaborative aaction research, intra-school as well as inter-schools
– the need for support by LEAs and other funding bodies for the movement of teacher as researcher
– the need for teachers to publish their findings, and for journals and other outlets that are geared towards classroom research as well as university or other funded research
– the need for networks to be established and widened to provide a forum and exchange mart for the ideas and innovatory practices of teachers

Synthesis stresses the need for careful validation (see Chapter 11). Does the study do what it set out to do? If not, why not? Is there sufficient evidence to back up claims? Can the public point to instances that act as this evidence? Is it presented in a clear form? Is there an account of the researcher's own progress and development as well as that of the clients'? These and many other related questions are all relevant.

This stage of the enquiry will produce some form of report which will then be made public. In organising the data in order to present the report, it is useful to retrace the steps of the action-reflection cycle. The inevitable retrospective element will not distort the interpretations if an on-going diary/reporting schedule of events and impressions has been kept.

*Retracing the steps*

| *Action research steps* | *Checklist* |
|---|---|
| I identify a problem when some of my educational values are denied in practice | – Is the problem clearly identified and stated?<br>– Are there other associated problem areas? Did others emerge during the enquiry? If so, was another action-reflection cycle set up, and is this clearly specified?<br>– Is there evidence to show the denial of values in practice? |
| I imagine a solution to the problem | – Is the solution clearly comprehensible?<br>– If there were alternative solutions, are reasons given for the choice of this particular one? |

| | |
|---|---|
| | – Is there evidence of the involvement of others? |
| I implement the solution | – Is there clear evidence to show this implementation?<br>– Have others been involved to monitor/evaluate the situation?<br>– Is there evidence to indicate the researcher's part in the enquiry? |
| I evaluate the outcome | – Is there a clear record of a validation process?<br>– Is this process accessible in documentary/other form?<br>– Is there now a systematic procedure for making it public?<br>– Does the solution actually solve the problem?<br>– Is there clear evidence of improvement?<br>– Is there clear evidence of the researcher's development? |
| I modify my solution in the light of my evaluation | – If such modification is necessary, are reasons given?<br>– Is the new plan clearly specified?<br>– Is the machinery ready again for a new action-reflection cycle? |

# Chapter 7

# Case Studies

## Introduction

Chapters 7, 8 and 9 are case studies. They are reports written by real teachers about their research into their own practice. Each report is an individual response to a particular problem of practice. Each captures the flavour of what it is like to be involved in trying to make sense of practice, of trying to improve practice, and of putting up with the constraints of the hurly-burly of school life. The reports tell of the pain and of the great satisfactions to be experienced when things finally go right, of the enormous insights to be gained through a critical look into the mirror.

Many significant aspects come to light in the studies. Perhaps the most obvious one is that of teacher education. Walker (1985) made the point that 'what is changed most by research is the researcher – it is almost always the researcher who learns most, changes most, has most commitment to the project and most at stake if it fails'. All three teachers here outline their honest attempts to remedy an unsatisfactory educational situation. Their victories are not without cost, yet their determination to carry out their own programme of systematic self-evaluation leaves them, and us, with a distinct feeling of satisfaction that an improvement of the educational situation has come about.

## Background to the reports

In April 1985, twenty-five teachers from Avon, Gloucester, Somerset and Wiltshire took part in a DES course entitled 'Supporting teachers in their classroom research'. The course was directed and coordinated by Jack Whitehead and Maureen Barrett of the School of Education, University of Bath. It was designed, so reads the handbook cover, 'to give you, the practitioners, an opportunity to investigate some aspect of your class practice more intensively than is normally possible'. The teachers met nine times over the year, five times at the School of Education and four times in teachers' centres or schools in the four educational authorities in July and October, 1985.

The course lasted officially for a year, until April 1986. Typical of such communities, most of the group maintain close links, and the research projects continue as vigorously as during the formal period of the course. Practitioners are still seeking answers to new questions, still keeping each other informed or asking support for their own enquiries. At the time of writing (1987) the network has expanded to include a part of the Avon TVEI Related In-Service Training (TRIST) programme on curriculum review and evaluation.

Much of what follows in the case studies comes from the journals of three of the teachers involved. Maureen Barrett writes in her open letter to the participants (1 July 1985): 'In these statements we have sensed a release of professional energy'; and Mike Parr says of the course (2 March 1986): '(it) has been an invaluable experience for me as it has offered me a practical and effective way to investigate and reflect upon my own classroom practice.'

## CASE STUDY 1

***Margaret Foy***

Selwood Middle School, Frome, Somerset

## Values into practice

*Introduction*

Margaret was concerned to encourage her children to take a greater responsibility for their own learning. Her account outlines her efforts to do so by adopting different teaching strategies to see which one might be most effective for this purpose. It is interesting how Margaret compares strategies, and decides, in collaboration with her children and other colleagues, which is most satisfactory for their particular educational needs.

When she was asked at the beginning of the course to write down her educational values, Margaret produced a daunting list.

> 'The values which are sound educational ones are synonymous for the teacher and pupils and I would like them to be used to judge both my professional practice and the performance of my pupils as teachers and learners.
> Reflective, thoughtful, confident, critical, self-critical, responsive, collaborative, discerning, responsible, evaluative, resolute, open-minded, tolerant, questioning, cooperative, sensitive,
> and have the ability to:
>
> research, record, discuss, to be rational, articulate well.'

She then identified reasons why she did not seem to be living out these values in class.

> I feel that children are too ready to sit in the classroom and absorb information like a sponge. I would like to set up a series of 'enterprises' which encouraged the children to set about embarking on these ideas with a view to evaluation of the language used. I feel that this type of approach is a necessary part of life itself in order to avoid exploitation, etc.

She spent much time discussing her problem and its possible solution with a colleague, who was later to observe several of her lessons and report back to Margaret and the whole group, part of a standard validation exercise. He writes of her educational concerns:

> Margaret is concerned with her students' developing a critical approach to learning and life in general. She feels that too often her students are content to be passive receivers of knowledge. This is not sufficient background for when they grow up and leave school. They need a critical, questioning approach in order that they can cope with life without exploitation. Margaret feels that this critical approach may be developed by students working on their own enterprises. This independent study will allow them to develop the values that Margaret feels are important.
>
> (22 April 1985)

Margaret takes up the story. She reflects on her identified educational values. 'I had to look carefully at myself within the classroom and ask which of these qualities I possessed and of those I did not, why not.

Why this list anyway? I realised that much of what I felt about how learning is achieved was rooted in my twelve years' experience in industry. Certainly I never learned anything without becoming involved in the process and certainly I never learned by being 'isolated' behind a desk. Therefore, why did I often teach without the children being directly involved? More reflections and the feeling was somewhat painful. Did I like playing to an audience? Was I being self-indulgent and getting satisfaction from how the children responded to me? Was I falling into the trap of 'pleasing the parents' by having the children produce written evidence of the work covered? Certainly my teaching felt prescriptive; and although the values I wrote down were met in some way they were often bypassed for expediency, syllabus restrictions, etc: and as an English teacher, too often I talked and the children wrote.

I had to plan out some strategies to satisfy my conviction that I could improve the way I taught and after all that was what I aimed to do. I put a toe in the water first with a group of children I knew well and had taught for a year. The results were interesting enough but made me realise that if I wanted to make any comparisons at all, I needed an idea with some uniformity in order to concentrate my observations of the diversity of the results.

PHASE ONE The second week of term I put my experiment into operation. Sadly I only had half the group from the year before, but knowing me, they proved to be the catalyst I needed. I am a firm believer in allowing the ideas I use to become part of my natural teaching life and as a result of this view I won't allow them to disrupt the general running of the school or cause stress to my overworked colleagues. Because I have a high regard for my head of department I tried to keep my experiments within the guidelines she had set down. With this in the background I set out my plan.

The children were 12+ (fourth-year middle school) and of the top ability range. There were thirty in the group, twelve boys and eighteen girls. They were allowed to choose their own groups provided they were mixed-sex groups. They split into four groups. I then handed out the following instructions:

1 Provide a script for a play.
2 Write out the dialogue.
3 Prepare and rehearse the play.
4 Present it.

I provided a prop box which would impose a thread common to each group. The box contained:

1 Old figured vase
2 Green evening dress
3 French sword (well sheathed)
4 A letter
5 An old family photograph
6 Silver snuff box

The children were to tape their conversations while they drew up their plans and their compulsory hour's homework entailed writing log books.

This being the only teacher input for five weeks, I then stood by and watched and kept a log myself. I emphasised to the children that there was no kind of assessment; that I was not so much interested in the end product but by what means they achieved it. During the next five weeks I found great difficulty in not interfering with what was going on. I felt guilty because I was doing no teaching, but I had to trust the children. I could have very easily changed my brief at this stage and written a psychological paper, because observing the group dynamics was absolutely fascinating. I was really both amazed and impressed with how most of the children reacted. Strangely enough the group who worked in my classroom could not work together at all and after three weeks I allowed them to move on to what proved to be the second stage of my experiment.

*My observations of this group*

(a) There were too many strong characters together (b) Their aims differed greatly (c) They were very intolerant of each other (d) They spent too much time changing their ideas

*Their observations*

> (a) John is being stupid. I'm not standing for it. (b) Peter says we wander from the point. (c) Our conversation turned into a debate on whether to believe in reincarnation or not. (d) I am learning to argue without actually getting angry. (e) I feel rather guilty and immature to think I failed the task. I don't think we were the right people to work together.

I consoled myself that if nothing else this group talked together, were reflective and self-critical.

As there were never more than eight children in my room, my lessons were spent wandering about the school observing them. I was totally amazed at how well they were aware of the school organisation.

*Quotes*

'We'll see the deputy Head. He has a room timetable.'
'Mrs Smith only uses the first-year hall every other Tuesday.'
'Mrs Jones has a battery-operated recorder.'
'The caretaker keeps the black plastic bags in . . . .'

They often wouldn't turn up to my room, but send a runner to say that they had organised a room with the deputy Head. They utilised benches, chairs and tables, which became thrones, police stations, etc. They wrote music, played the piano, flute, clarinet; made costumes and wrote their scripts. Finally for each other they presented their plays. I was delighted with what I saw. Many of the values I put forward were present in their work.

The children's quotes are perhaps a valuable guide to this:

*Sharon*, Day 4: At least we got something down on paper.
Day 7: I realised today that working in a group is very valuable. It made me realise that whatever I do I will have to work with someone else. I don't think talking is a waste of time as we have time to air our views.

*Michael*: I think this is a very good idea because it gives us the responsibility of producing something with an end product – all in all a good week's work!

*Julie*: Unfortunately I had the afternoon off. We had to decide to allow people to ad lib so we don't stop to sort out mistakes.

At this point in this group's play their 'star' became ill and gave prior notice she would be away the day they were to perform their play.

*Mary* (the star): I was away so Valerie is taking my part – I am the curtain puller. (No hard feelings.)

By now the children had become very sensitive to each other's feelings and 'the play' became important – not themselves – to my mind a very significant step forward. The differences between how the boys and girls approached the project was very interesting. In all but one group the girls led. They organised the group, providing scripts for me to photocopy, brought in props, wrote songs and disciplined the boys with whom they worked. In the group where the boys led, the girls (naturally quiet ones) still did much of the organisational side, but it was delegated by the two boys who were 'ideas men'.

Having gone this far I still wasn't satisfied. The word 'inefficient' kept appearing subliminally in my head. It was at this stage I decided the way forward.

1 I would set another experiment with more teacher input.
2 I would take the children into my confidence completely.
3 I would do a third experiment.
4 I would ask them to assess the methods of teaching and to comment and reflect upon them.

PHASE TWO The second project was based on the book *Elidor* by Alan Garner. Our normal approach to novels is a mixture of teaching styles with a large number of worksheets covering the many English activities concerned with reading, writing and oral work. I have my doubts about worksheets anyway and the term 'learning by correspondence' which my husband uses seems very apt. I settled for a mixture of group work and individual work.

1 The individual work was to be their hour's homework. This was to be a diary of reactions to the book itself plus any observations they wished to make about their classwork.
2 Their group work was merely based on the one instruction 'see where the book leads you'.

For the next five weeks the children explored the novel and allowed it to dictate what their activities were. I merely acted as facilitator and mentor – that is, providing any materials they asked for, settling disagreements (which had often delayed work in their first projects), suggesting improvements and reading their copious notes. I had suggested maybe they could write or needed to write a couple of sides of 9cm by 7cm for each chapter, but it was entirely their decision – most of them did!

At the end of the five weeks I was delighted and surprised by what they had produced.

They had captured the wonder, the fear, the magic of *Elidor* in so many ways.

1 Fiona and Mark produced an adventure book based on 'Dungeons and Dragons'.
2 Four girls produced a miscellany of poems, word searches, drawings, puzzles, questions and answers, a synopsis of each chapter, games (in all about 100 sheets).
3 Four boys did a computer game which they hope to have published by the county computer magazine (I saw nothing of them for five weeks except when I went to the computer room).
4 A series of pictures plus a tape of the story was done by another mixed group.

Other things submitted were: jigsaw puzzle, various adventure games, a game which involved a visual answer (that is, painted or drawn), a question-type game. In addition they all produced very comprehensive diaries giving me tremendous insight into what the novel meant to them. They took sides with various characters, they identified with certain characters, and they had learned to appreciate the writing of Alan Garner.

At the end two more words were added to my 'values list' – inventive and innovatory!

One boy asked if he could approach his written work in a different way. He produced a ballad, in verses of four lines, on the whole book. Previously he had resented writing anything at all.

I must say at this stage I felt very humble. I felt I had seriously misunderstood the ability of the children I taught.

PHASE THREE I set up the final experiment without the children realising what was involved. It was a four-week series of lessons which had very carefully worked out 'content' and in which I was the main 'protagonist'. The lessons were all centred around different types of reading; whereas normally there would be discussions at this time, I explained and they worked. At the end of the four weeks, I told them the whole story of how I had set up the lessons to find out their reactions. I talked with them about learning and how we learn, and then asked them to write down their reactions. I think perhaps the way to evaluate my classroom research is to let the children have their say.

*Anne*: Working as a group we work better; the class respond when the teacher is fun to be with. In this kind of situation pupils learn and take things in without realising it. You can learn without pressure.

*Peter*: I like it when the teacher helps you a little bit, gets you started, and helps you when you go wrong.

*Melanie*: With a teacher teaching you all the time you may learn more, but it's very boring. Saying things in front of the whole class is different from saying things in a small group.

*Lucy*: If you had a good job like being a doctor or a dentist then you wouldn't normally have someone in a higher position saying "make sure you do this or that". It makes you a little more confident.

*David*: I like working in groups with enough help to make sure you don't make mistakes yet without being over-restricted on what you can do.

*Matthew*: Group teaching is probably very difficult for the teacher, but they will most likely get better results from it.

*Sharon*: Children can speak freely without a teacher nagging at them – groups are adventurous.

*Julie*: Part of life is working with groups of people and cooperation. It was a way of preparing us when in the future you're put into an ocean of people without a life raft.

The general consensus was that a classroom where the teacher acted as facilitator was the best, but most of the children could see that a variety of teaching styles may be necessary. Two of the girls from the original group who could not agree or work together actually preferred the didactic method of teaching.

*Jane*: Pupils learn more because you are forever pumping things into them. Even though it is boring I think it's better.

*Jean*: I like the teacher at the front teaching grammar. This way no one can make an excuse why they don't know the work.

Both of these children are pushed by successful parents who want them to succeed. Their written work is very comparable to 'meatless sandwiches' – nicely proportioned, but without filling. Both girls are highly competitive and are involved in guides, music, ballet, etc. I remember asking Jean about reading. She told me that she loved it, but didn't have time. They have no feeling for language and are not interested in it intrinsically, merely as a tool – what a challenge for me!

*Summary*

The views of the children on the work done were very illuminating, but how did I feel? I felt that the first phase that I carried out lacked guidelines. I felt that more teacher involvement was necessary. The children worked well, but two of the groups could have had a better end product, and therefore more satisfaction, if I had stepped in and guided them. The tapes I listened to gave the impression of a 'think tank'. The ideas bounced around like rubber balls, but they never succeeded in catching them and holding fast. The one group who did hold fast were wise enough to take a simple idea that was well within their grasp and, using their talents, produce a worthwhile production.

Like the children, I favoured Phase Two. Here I issued guidelines and then 'hovered'. I listened and watched and unobtrusively intervened with suggestions and support. I was able to settle disputes and put different points of view. Although the written work was imposed, I found that because of the freedom to express ideas in other ways the children happily wrote up their points of view on the novel they were studying.

Looking back, the whole experience was very rewarding and I certainly learned more about classroom practice. I think that my approach to preparation will be different: my attitude more relaxed towards the way the lessons go. I had always been meticulous and I always envisaged the 'amount' of work to be done. Now I feel I will still have an end in view, but the route taken will be far more pupil navigated and I feel the 'amount' will be surpassed as a result of enthusiasm and not pressure. My next task will be to see how I can apply these techniques to my geography lessons which are with mixed-ability classes and following a syllabus agreed on with the Upper School.

Phase Three, the didactic teaching experiment, was done not for my own interest (I knew which way I wanted to go), but for the children's experience and comment. It would be wrong to say that the children hated it or that I certainly loved it, but the point was did the children learn in the way I felt necessary? As I looked around the room I was aware that many were not 'wired in for sound' even though specific ideas were being put forward, whereas in Phase Two the children were actively involved in their own learning.

At the beginning I wondered if I possessed the qualities which I regarded as important in my pupils. Could they be used as a yardstick to assess my classroom practice? I was certainly 'questioning, cooperative, tolerant, open-minded, resolute' – but 'reflective, thoughtful, confident, critical, self-critical, responsive, sensitive, and evaluative'? Perhaps not.

This study has certainly made me aware of the need to possess these qualities and to encourage them in my pupils, because these are the qualities which encourage the children to be responsible and involved in what they are learning. I became a partner and learned with the children and they in turn appreciated my knowledge and experience. Let me quote one of the children here:

> The work we do in class is good as long as it is interesting and Mrs Foy definitely keeps everyone's interest. You can learn without pressure. Ideas flow like gushing water.

I realised, too, that I was far too interested in the 'end product' and didn't monitor the process by which the children learned. It is often by following and observing the direction of a child's learning pattern that the teacher can be most useful, assisting the child when he needs it.

I think many of the children felt that they had learned better because they were motivated to do so. The motivation was being able to implement their own ideas in a way which they understood.

All the children deserve my thanks for their cooperation and so do the staff who supported my work.'

AUTHOR'S NOTE

In personal correspondence, Margaret Foy recounts how her research study is moving forward her own school policy. She says:

> My headmaster and my head of department are very supportive of what I would like to happen in the classroom. Since doing the research, we have tried to incorporate many of the techniques into the teaching of English to the 11+ and 12+ pupils . . . Without exception they prefer to work in this way.

J. M., March 1987

# Chapter 8

## CASE STUDY 2

*Zita Gisborne*
Charlton Kings School, Cheltenham, Gloucestershire

## Evaluating my teaching in dress and textiles

*Introduction*

Zita's report is a gem which will surely touch the heart of all teachers. It is easy to identify with her desire to involve her children in their own learning, with her dismay when her efforts are frustrated, with her eagerness to improve her own performance. Her report shows courage and the tacit conviction that things can be made better, even though the odds seem sometimes unfairly stacked.

*Background information including my professional concerns*

During the early stages of the course I found difficulty in clarifying in my own mind which of my educational concerns were to be paramount and which discounted, at least for the present.

On 22 April 1985, I stated that although I had been actively involved with workshops and committees discussing curriculum development in school, I had become frustrated by the lack of action. Recognising that the main reason for this was because of 'problems related to the re-organisation of schools in the country', I decided to confine my energies to an area over which I have some control and look at my own classroom teaching. As a head of a Dress and Textiles department and moderator for coursework for CSE, I am concerned about the 'process' as well as the 'product' of the educational experience for pupils.

Having also been involved in discussion about this with colleagues teaching the subject, it is apparent that there is growing disquiet about the way textiles has become fragmented and devalued. Variously titled needlework, needlecraft, dressmaking, fashion or creative textiles, its validity as part of the school curriculum appears to be in doubt. Added to this is the traditional view of textiles as being primarily about 'sewing' and the way in which it is tugged in two directions either by Art or Home Economics departments in secondary schools.

On 22 June 1985 we were all invited to define our educational values. This was for me a most difficult task. I had still no definite idea about which aspects of my classroom practice I should be studying, except a vague idea that it should be about the use of new curriculum material which promotes group and individual experiential learning. My statement at that time seems now to have been rather muddled and much of it was coloured by emotion rather than cold professional judgement.

One comment which I have had cause to review in the light of discussion with colleagues on the course was, 'Teacher accountability is very important, but unless others are sympathetic to your educational values . . . problems may arise.' More importantly I had at the time allowed criticism of my teaching methods (based on the fact that I was not teaching traditional sewing) to be confused with apparent criticism of my educational aims and my professional abilities. I went on to say that 'educational values in a "practical" subject are just as important as in an academic one and that I am not merely concerned with imparting knowledge or training in hand skills'.

Two other phrases which now seem to have more significance are, 'In order to achieve a good working relationship in the classroom I believe that negotiation between pupils, teacher and parents is important' and 'My main concern is to allow pupils to develop a sense of judgement about and responsibility for their own practical and creative work within the classroom situation'. I felt it important enough to attempt to hold a meeting with parents of the children in the fourth year who were embarking on a two-year course in textiles leading to either CSE Needlecraft which has a large coursework component, or GCE 'O' level in Needlework and Dress. As can be seen, even examination boards cannot agree the title and therefore the craft bias of the subject.

*Course of action*

Having gone through the process of working out my concerns and educational values I sought to identify three areas for concern:

1 negotiation between pupils, parents and teacher;
2 pupils' responsibility for their own practical/creative work;
3 provide a short basic course on textiles which would encourage pupils to work in groups, while applying the knowledge gained to their individual projects, in order to develop skills other than 'craft' skills.

In order to examine these areas more closely I decided to:

1 seek my headmaster's approval for a meeting with parents, to which their child was also to be welcomed;
2 spend a whole session (four lessons: 35 minutes split after the first by lunch) having a team-teaching/discussion presentation. This entailed showing examples of a wide range of completed textile work, giving syllabi content and coursework requirements and group discussions on individual projects. Pupils were also to be told that they could choose their working groups and teacher and that this could be changed in future by mutual agreement;
3 select and use as appropriate curriculum material from the Nuffield-Chelsea: Home Economics Basic Course – Textiles and Fabrics 14–16. Having used some of this material in the first and fifth year during the academic year 1984–85 I had already become familiar with the content, but not necessarily the problems.

At the end of the summer term after a particularly useful 'tutorial' at Swindon, I had refined my strategies and obtained my headmaster's permission to invite parents to a meeting, although he was doubtful of the value of such a meeting. In order to gain more from this meeting than a one–off discussion, I also had in mind to write to parents again after examination time and ask for their reactions to the value of the course and apparent achievement of their child. However, this was beyond the scope of the present investigation, but is still something I would like to do.

My main strategies for obtaining feedback and monitoring the degree of success for points 1 and 2 were:

(a) use radio microphones and videorecorder to obtain information about the pupil involvement and participation in lessons:

(b) request help from my colleague to observe pupil involvement and participation. (This meant that we would have all 28 pupils in one room for one or two lessons of the session and when applicable split them into groups according to the material to be presented. She was asked to accept a series of lessons and methods of teaching about which she has certain reservations.)

(c) keep a careful check on the connections between the 'theory' and 'practice' by constantly referring to the basic textiles course and asking pupils to keep diaries and be prepared to evaluate their own projects and discuss 'success' and 'failures' with their group.

(d) keep my own journal of the course as it progressed.

### *The investigation – 4 September to 23 October 1985*

#### THE SCHOOL

An 11–16 secondary school in Cheltenham, with a fifth/sixth-form entry. The fourth year is particularly large because of the closure of another school in the locality. In the past two years we have absorbed approximately 70 extra pupils; over 30 this September. There is a rotation scheme of eight to nine subjects (practical) in the first and second year with a 'mini' option of two terms of three subjects in the third year. Pupils must take two of these in the fourth/fifth year.

#### THE PUPILS

Of the 180 pupils in the fourth year 97 are girls. Boys do not often opt for 'sewing'. There are 42 girls taking one of the two textiles subjects offered:

28 Needlecraft 14 Embroidery

Of the 28 girls in the fourth-year needlecraft group only seventeen had been in this school up to the third year and two of these had joined us in the course of the third year. Of the remainder all but one had come from one local school. The one 'odd' pupil had not only never had to take any aesthetic/practical subject, but had been placed in my area 'because I was the only teacher who had room for her apart from woodwork'. Nevertheless she said she was 'willing to give it a try'.

*The curriculum project – Fibres/yarns/fabrics*

To make some attempt to justify my belief in my professional concerns and educational values by:

1 evaluating a half-term course of lessons on the basic raw materials used in textiles and the processes through which they are converted into consumer goods;
2 attempting to clarify the vocabulary of the subject in order to help pupils to be more specific while encouraging concept development;
3 provide a clear 'design brief' – for example, 'the use of fine/soft/semi-transparent fabric' which would greatly limit the function/style/technique of the project so that the learning of 'theory' was more relevant.

*The lessons*
*(Using microscopes, room library, worksheets and quizzes.)*

1 As projected; more on 'sales pitch' than usual because of the mixed experience of the group. Told about study!
2 Words and misconceptions: cotton instead of thread/fabric; wool for knitted articles instead of yarn, etc.
3 Dissecting fabrics to break down to basic raw material.
4 Fibre classification (family groups).
5 Flow chart from previous lesson and origins.
6 Practical construction workshop (i) hand knitting, (ii) machine knitting, (iii) spinning, (iv) weaving.
7 Discussion of previous work. Crossword.
8 Discussion groups.

*What actually happened*

(a) Having invited parents to a meeting by sending an approved letter home between 4 and 11 September, only one reply slip was returned – a positive reply, but the only one. I had to chase all the rest (thirteen) and all but two gave no particular reason for not being able or even wishing to come. (C's parents came without her, but were very understanding and supportive.)

(b) Unable (or perhaps unwilling?) to obtain radio-microphones. Room too large and echo presents problems for any other type.

(c) Video recording only of limited success because of organisational problems. I wrote at the time:

> 16 October 1985 Video: Matthew and Tony (the fifth-year boys currently responsible for use of video on projects): had too many problems obtaining the video and operators. Despite agreeing originally to 'free' the boys from lessons one member of staff retracted. Time changed.
>
> 23 October 1985 Video: Matthew and Tony, as you were! I give up . . . All lessons on Wednesday morning cancelled (due to lack of interest?) Union action. Muddle over booking. Can't cope!

(d) I decided between lessons six and seven to demonstrate the use of the knitting machine. This left less time for other work.

(e) I felt that at the end of the course, in view of the fact that as I had personally missed the most 'active' and undirected lesson, it would be an advantage to present pupils with a questionnaire. There were also two other occasions when classes were depleted because of 'action', so I had not had the time for discussion at the end of the course with pupils as planned.

(f) My colleague and I both started these lessons almost every week under a great deal of pressure. Because of 'travelling' time, changing rooms and lack of ancillary help, we both chased round on 'physical' problems and felt that this started the lessons badly for the pupils. Comments such as, 'There is little time to organise lessons between classes', 'No possibility of leaving projector out – form room and evening institute', 'Preparation/evaluation/discussion time lacking', are sprinkled liberally over the notes I made during the eight weeks.

(g) We also found ourselves disagreeing about the degree to which pupils were achieving the desired goals of personalising their educational experience and because of this we were also frustrated by the lack of time to get together with the material and discuss changes. However, one area upon which we were agreed was that it was a struggle to get the pupils to talk to us! At the beginning we had been encouraged by the way in which they had organised their groups; we stipulated only that the 'new' pupils should distribute themselves evenly, which they did. As the weeks went by, we became concerned that this may be more apathy than social unease.

> 18 September 1985 Given worksheet on microscopes, but all had to be chivied to use them. 'Found some could not recognise

difference between dissection and destruction.' 'Concerned about D, E, F and C – non-communicative.' 'A and B very quiet, but obviously have gained understanding because when PINNED DOWN – they know!'

3 October 1985 Placed tables together. Asked to make cards (words). Memory–books–use of index. Each group given one 'family'. Large display at end bringing all groups together. Very active, but small group from 'O' rather lost; they do not like the uncertainty. C spent time staring into space. No comment from her; her group is not verbally active anyway. H is a reliable prop!

(h) Pupils are asking for more support in the supply of written information: 'We need notes.' More provided.

*Reflections*

Perhaps the most difficult task for me over the last few weeks has been to overcome my own feelings of inadequacy. I became almost obsessed by the 'failure' of my attempt to involve the parents. This and a growing lack of self-confidence over the last year had meant that my view of what had actually occurred was very one-sided. Self-interest is self-defeating.

Although I may have had pressures upon me which were affecting my vision of my professional abilities, within the classroom this was not evident. Happily, Maureen together with three colleagues on the course were able between them to push me towards a realisation of what was happening. In all the confusion I had lost sight of those for whom I work – the pupils.

So how much of what I had attempted (rather too much I now acknowledge) had had the desired effect?

*The parents*

On the positive side, one set of parents let me know that they cared for their daughter. They obviously felt the 'subject' of sufficient worth to merit giving up an evening of their time to discuss the way she would be taught. I know that they want their daughter to do well and for them that means gaining sufficient knowledge, understanding and skills to obtain a good examination result. They also stated that whatever happened, as long as we both tried and she enjoyed the course the time was not wasted.

*The pupils*

The achievement of pupils in these lessons cannot be measured by examination results or test scores. We did not hold any tests or examinations.

One obvious measure of success or achievement is the final product of the project work. However, I have stated that this is not my only concern; the process by which the individual arrives at the product is of equal importance and cannot be so easily assessed.

Nevertheless, the video tape did show that despite some members of the class appearing to be rather passive, when encouraged to become involved, most of the TALK was subject centred and not gossip. This would indicate that a degree of involvement was growing and I have been encouraged by the way this has progressed since.

There has been a general movement between the two basic groups. No one had been 'left out' and when a pupil decides that she wants to go and work with a different group or in a different room there has been consultation with peers and a request to the teacher (totally unsolicited), 'Do you mind if I go next door?' My colleague and I have both observed this and have only on one occasion had to change the groups ourselves to avoid time wasting.

Pupils are beginning to use a more specific vocabulary and transferable skills are more evident. They are urging us (the teachers) to provide for their needs. This independence is as yet shown in less than half the class, but it is encouraging.

The provision of graphic or written information to 'back up' work was a consequence of a general plea for revision notes. Many pupils felt that not only were they expected to have good reliable memories, but that I was failing to do my job as a teacher. Teachers are expected to make pupils write.

I have on the negative side to state that there has been only a slight change in the pupils' attitudes to the subject. They still want to refer to their 'sewing' as being the most important aspect. More work on integrating the theory with the practical needs to be done before they are likely to see time spent away from 'sewing' as being no intrusion.

Certainly I have found that the pupils found some of the work difficult. There is evidence, however, to show that they don't always appreciate having to think for themselves. Nor do they like what they see as a failure on my part to tell them when instructions are not correct!

The group working with the knitting machine 'failed' to get it to knit. The instructions were faulty (manufacturer not teacher.) This led to a good-humoured discussion during the demonstration and the video shows an animated, if not heated, argument about my responsibilities towards them. 'But you should have known it was wrong and told us.' 'You let us get in a mess.' This was a golden opportunity to reinforce my reasons for encouraging them to rely less heavily on the infallibility of the teacher because I had not noticed the error myself.

I must also acknowledge that over the last year I have experienced exactly those feelings of uncertainty that my pupils have. Taking away the formal, traditionally accepted modes of learning based on teacher dependence and replacing it with the autonomy to decide your own means to an end, leaves a great big hole. There is also the feeling common to myself and my pupils that time could have been saved by using traditionally accepted ways. But there is a happy medium and I am not too sure whether I have got it right yet.

Finally, I offer the following comments as evidence that, despite my conviction that what I am doing is beginning to show results, the pupils still seem to have reservations; although one pupil who had come to these classes 'fresh' as it were, was quite genuine, I felt, when she said at the end of the discussion, 'It's a lot better than I thought it was going to be, and although I may not be able to gain enough skills (techniques) in the time left before exams to enter, at least it won't be wasted.'

*Extracts from conversation with six pupils 24 February 1986*

Three had been at school from the first year; two had entered in the third year; one had entered in the fourth year. In response to criticisms expressed in answer to questionnaires, I asked if they would mind telling me about their feelings about and understanding of (a) the seven week course on fibres, and (b) the way in which they were being asked to approach their project work.

The following pupils' comments were noted:

1 Why can't you just show us all one way to do something?
2 Why can't you give us more information sheets about what we are doing?
3 When you tell me there is a way to do something, you make me look it up in a book. Sometimes I get the wrong book or it doesn't appear in the index and I get frustrated because I waste time.

4 You and Mrs M often tell us things differently and that is confusing.
5 When we did those lessons on fibres and things you spent too long on some for me. I got bored.
6 We could have learned all that by copying from books in half the time.
7 I do still remember most of that though so perhaps it was a good way of doing it. I don't think I would take it in from books.
8 Why can't we have one textbook and use it for all our work. You could tell us which chapters to look up and answer questions like in our other lessons.

My comments to them were:

They must begin to use their own judgement about 'best' tools, methods, etc. Life is about making choices. We can only make sound choices if decisions are based on good background information.

They had already informed me that there were some areas in the course where they were feeling the lack of information. As stated, I provided information sheets more regularly and systematically after this.

The comments on time were most helpful. Both Mrs M and I had felt that although we were under pressure in an organisational way, much of the work needed to be more structured to take account of the variety of experience, previous knowledge and ability. We have resolved to make time to cooperate on planning a much more structured course for the remainder of the year.

# Chapter 9

## CASE STUDY 3

***Mike Parr***
Bath Technical College, Bath, Avon

## How can I evaluate my teaching in Engineering Technology?

*Introduction*

Mike's report shows clearly how he adopted an action-reflection spiral in his attempts to evaluate his teaching in engineering technology. It is interesting to see how he focuses progressively on problem issues, and how he adopts one strategy and rejects it in favour of a better one. His desire to involve others in his study – first his students and then a research collaborator – is a hallmark of his openness and willingness to make public his systematic enquiry into his own educational development.

This report sets out to describe the developments that have taken place in the investigation I have undertaken in my own classroom practice as a Lecturer in Electronics at the City of Bath Technical College through my participation in the DES-funded course held at Bath University, 'Supporting teachers in their classroom practice'. It does not set out to present in detail the evidence that I have collected so far, but to describe the process by which this course was able to offer me an insight into the way I might begin to develop a systematic research method appropriate to my particular classroom experiences and concerns.

*Concerns relating to full-time students in the Engineering Technology department at Bath Technical College*

(a) COURSE AND STUDENT DETAILS

Two year full-time
BTEC Certificate in Electronics
Entry qualifications: minimum 3 CSE. Many have 'O' levels
10 to 15 students per class, two classes per year
Approximately 27 hours spent in college per week
Course divided into 'units' each of 60 hours length lasting 9 or 18 weeks. 15 to 20 units over the two years
Age range 16–20 years, mostly male
Each unit may be taught by two or three lecturers over a year. They may come into contact with ten teachers
There are no tutorial sessions
They are not issued with books and few students purchase them
They may spend five to seven hours in the lab each week

(b) MY CONCERNS (APRIL 1985)

I am experiencing dissatisfaction with my method of teaching. I am an imparter of information, the students are subjected to long periods of note taking. They are passive. I feel that this leads the students to becoming disinterested and bored. I would like to change to a resource-based learning approach, but feel constrained by the way the course is organised and the attitudes of my colleagues. We need to get together to look closely at the needs of the students.

(c) INVESTIGATION OF STUDENT ATTITUDES (23 APRIL 1985)

I sent the students out of the classroom for a few minutes and in the meantime I had written out the questions shown below. On their return they immediately began to interest themselves in it and started a discussion amongst themselves and with me which led us on to a discussion of some of the terms used and the roles of teachers and learners and the importance of good learning experiences.

*The questions they were asked to reply to in their own time*

Describe your learning at Bath Tech.

(1) Why did you come on to the course?

(2) What is it like to be a 'learner' on this course? (describe good and bad aspects – likes/dislikes)
(3) How does this experience compare with (a) school, (b) your expectations of what you thought the course would be like?
(4) Describe one good and one bad learning experience at the college.

Try and be frank and honest. Your replies should be anonymous.

*Summaries of replies: 8 replied out of a possible 18*

Most thought that a good learning experience was when you enjoyed the subject and it is made interesting, when you are able to do things for yourself.

Most thought that relationships with teachers were better than at school: 'more relaxed', 'treated as equals', 'more freedom'.

Most thought that long sessions of note taking were not enjoyable and liked when they were involved in what was going on; for example, practical work and discussions in class. Dictation of notes was generally disliked. 'While you are writing things down you cannot be understanding what is said.' Some thought that teaching at the Tech was generally of a higher standard than at school.

*Statement of my educational values (12 June 1985)*

1 Students and teachers are equal in human terms.
2 The educational environment should reflect value 1.
3 My own classroom practice should reflect value 1.
4 Students and teachers should be equal participants in the classroom.
5 I should enable the students to take more responsibility for their own learning.
6 The students should become more aware of the learning process and the part they are expected to play in it.
7 Expecting nothing of students except to receive knowledge and then to regurgitate it on demand is a form of oppression. Education should equip people with the means by which they are able to liberate themselves from oppression.
8 Students should be equal participants in the learning process.
9 Learning should be a meaningful and enjoyable experience.

10 The learning process should involve the social interaction between students and between students and teachers.

*Academic year starting September 1985*

My original intention had been to try and realise my educational values within the classroom setting by adopting a student-centred learning approach. My reasons for this were as follows:

I feel that I can relate to students on a more equal footing if they are actively involved in their own learning process. In that way they will gain confidence in themselves as 'learners', rather than the receivers of information from a person who is 'better' than they are. This means that they are involved in a real educational process which they will be able to benefit from after they leave the College.

Another important factor is the way I respond to them as individuals and the way that they perceive my role as a teacher. I feel that their expectations of me as the source of all their knowledge, and therefore superior to them, is reinforced by the 'chalk and talk' style of teaching. This creates a barrier which makes it difficult for me to realise my educational values. Removing this barrier may help me to become an enabler of a learner environment which can be tailored to their needs, not just in the narrow sense of learning about electronics, but also in the wider context of building up their confidence in their ability to learn for themselves.

However, the way that my timetable had been arranged for this academic year meant that I was no longer teaching this group of full-time students in the classroom, but only saw them in their practical and project work sessions. I saw this originally as a problem because I felt that this way was the environment more suited to them and I saw no apparent conflict of my educational values arising. I had also gained evidence from their written replies, in response to the questions I had asked them in relation to their learning experience at the College, that they very much enjoyed the practical sessions. But on closer examination of this situation through discussions that took place on the DES course I was able to reflect on this and ask several questions that I thought would move me forward in a way that would help me in my investigations. I quote from points that I made on 7 November 1985:

It has been interesting for me to observe one particular group who I have previously taught in a standard classroom situation last term. It was this experience that led me to question my classroom practice and examine alternative approaches. I now see the group solely in the laboratory where they undertake practical/project work which is designed not only to develop their practical skills, but to reinforce what they learn in class. Their level of activity is much higher and they are able to maintain this for periods up to three hours and it is sometimes difficult to get them out of the door at the end! This contrasts with their all too apparent boredom in the classroom and their inability under those circumstances to concentrate for periods longer than half an hour out of a two-hour period. In the lab they are able to work at their own pace and I am able to give individual attention to those students who need it.

*The questions I need to ask*

1 Why is it that they apparently enjoy the periods spent in the lab much more than in the classroom?
2 Does this apparent enjoyment mean that they are more able to learn?
3 Would it be possible for me to integrate this type of learning into the course as part of and not separate from classroom-based learning?

I felt that I was now beginning to get somewhere in that I was pinpointing my concerns and maybe a direction in which I would be able to improve the quality of the student's learning experience. But I was still at a loss to see what I was to do next. How, for instance, was I to discover what the quality and extent of their learning was? Could I be certain that their concept of learning coincided with mine? Obviously I would have to undertake a more systematic and detailed investigation of, first, the present situation and, second, make some changes and monitor the effect of them.

At this point a postgraduate student at Bath University, Alan Skelton, was undertaking his own research into the educational values of teachers and the possible conflicts that were occurring in their classroom practice. He was introduced to me through the enquiry network that was now established at the University of Bath, and I agreed to collaborate with him in a series of video sessions with follow-up discussions and interviews with the students. This was to make an enormous impact on the progress that I would make in carrying out my own investigation as it would, apart from other advantages, relieve me from a lot of the practical problems of arranging for videos to be made, etc. The other advantages were that a regular series of discussions enabled me to clarify many of my original statements and concerns.

The first video turned out, due to technical difficulties, a disappointment (something that should be expected quite often I have discovered!) which left me with a feeling of uncertainty still. The reasons I discussed with Maureen Barrett on 22.11.85, and were as follows.

What was I going to get from the video? Was the video going to take over and impose restrictions rather than enable me to get a clearer picture of what goes on in my classes? Second, an equally important problem had arisen in that Alan could not observe me on the days that I would be teaching the full-time group who were the focus of my original concerns and would take as a subject the other CSE Electronics class who I only see for two hours a week. I felt that I would need to rethink my whole approach to the investigation. On reflection this has not been the major problem I first perceived it as.

Taking the second point first it has become clear to me that establishing a statement of educational values acts as a framework around which an investigation can be built. The educational values are a constant reference point and do not change according to the class being taught (although they may be extended and modified for the sake of clarity). So the fact that I was now focusing on the second group did not mean that I would have to ignore my original concerns since my concerns relate to my educational values and apply to any group of students. Any changes I would wish to make or any conclusions I draw would apply equally well to any group of students that I teach.

With reference to the problem perceiving the usefulness of the video, once again viewing with the educational values in mind helps in gaining valuable information about the classroom. Are my values being lived out in the classroom or lab? Is it of use to determine which values are being realised and which of them are not? This way it would be possible, at the very least, to gain an insight into the exact nature of my concerns because these concerns stem from a non-realisation of some of those values. The video is only one way by which evidence may be collected. The use of independent observers and my own impressions, reinforced with interviews with the students and discussions with the educational values in mind, is a very powerful investigative tool which can reveal a wealth of information.

*Evidence gained through observation of the electronics class at Bath Technical College*

INFORMATION ABOUT THE GROUP

They are students from a local boys comprehensive school who are in the Lower Sixth and are retaking CSEs and 'O' levels. They attend the College two half days a week taking a mode three CSE Electronics course. I only see them for two hours, another member of staff having them for the rest of the time.

They exhibit the same problem that I observed with the full-time classes in not being able to concentrate for very long in the classroom 'theory' sessions and have always expressed a preference for practical work. Many of them have the disadvantage of being made to come to College and are not that interested in Electronics as a subject. Having said that, however, they make the best of it and I feel an additional responsibility to make the subject as enjoyable as possible for them.

THE INVESTIGATION SO FAR

To date three out of five videos have been technically successful and two of those have been discussed in detail. One questionnaire was carried out with students giving their responses in the classroom. Alan has also conducted and tape recorded interviews with a number of the students referring them to instances from the videos. A programme has now been developed whereby a video is made one week with a follow-up analysis and the next week the students are interviewed.

The videos and Alan's observations have revealed several important points about the class. First, they spend a large proportion of the time used in the laboratory 'on task'. They are active participants in that they ask questions frequently. Second, I spend a great deal of my time talking to the students about their work and also about things not related directly to their work. This I see as a realisation of several of my values. I am, however, uncertain as to the amount of responsibility they take for their own learning – I am still seen as the one person who has all the answers although I try to get them to look at their notes.

The questionnaire was not very productive, the students' responses being short and to some extent flippant. This, to a large extent, can be attributed to the way it was introduced to the class, it being hurried and without a full explanation of what the purpose of the investigation was.

The interviews with the students bear a marked contrast to this. The students come over as being very aware of their impressions of the classroom. They are articulate and appear to be taking an interest in the investigation.

To give one example: this is a section of a transcript taken from a recording where Alan is asking a student, John, about his feelings about a session spent investigating logic circuits using 'Logic Tutors' which enable the student to connect various logic circuits and to observe, by the use of light emitting diodes (leds), the response of the circuits to changes in input conditions. From this they are able to construct a 'truth table' and compare it against the table derived from 'theory'. I had introduced the theory the previous week and the aim was that they would need to refer back to this information for confirmation of the validity of their experimental results. By this means I was aiming to enable them to extend and deepen their understanding of the topic through the practical work.

> *A. S.*: Right, then, I want to know how you felt about having the Logic Tutors actually in the classroom like that.
>
> *John*: Well . . . no matter how old you are it's fun to have something to play with (both laugh) . . . it's practical . . . you've got something that shows light so it's I don't know . . . it was better like that, it was more interesting because you got a result from what you were doing for yourself (*A. S.*: Yes, when you were doing the truth tables) rather than someone telling you what's going to happen . . . if you get them wrong, you've got to work out why it is . . . I reckon it's much more interesting that way.
>
> *A. S.*: And can you think of a way of actually doing it . . . to look at that theory of logic gates, can you think of a way that you'd like to do it?
>
> *John*: No, not really, that was the best way I thought you could do it. Because you do it yourself you not only learn more, but it's more interesting than somebody standing at the front and telling you what's going on.

I think it is worth adding here that John is a student who has expressed his reluctance to being on the course and would like to spend the time on subjects he is more interested in.

*In conclusion*

Time does not permit me at this stage to go into a fuller presentation of the evidence, but I hope it gives the flavour of the investigation that I am presently involved in. The DES course 'Supporting teachers in their classroom research' has been an invaluable experience for me as it has offered me a practical and effective way to investigate and reflect upon my own classroom practice. Through participating with fellow course members it has extended the network of teachers undertaking similar enquiries through which we are able to provide mutual support and guidance.

# PART III

# IMPLICATIONS

# Chapter 10

# Questions and Answers about Action Research

## Introduction

Action researchers are deliberately encouraging change. Any form of change is unsettling and controversial, and some questions about the research design and results are sure to arise.

The comments below are direct quotations or paraphrases of reactions from people who challenge the notion of action research. It is a fair assumption that anyone reading this book will hear several of the comments during the course of his or her own study.

QUESTION 1 What you are doing could never be described as 'research'. Certainly you are considering your own practice, continually taking stock and seeking to improve your own teaching performance, but that is what good teachers should be doing anyway. That is not research.

ANSWER You are aware of at least half my practice. Yes, I am continually taking stock and seeking to improve my own performance, as you say. What you do not acknowledge, however, is that I am also monitoring my performance in a systematic way, and making my findings public. I am following through what Lawrence Stenhouse calls 'a systematic enquiry made public' (1980). I am keeping detailed records of what I do in class, and what my children do. My children also keep records. All this written evidence is there for you to see, as well as for anyone else who wishes to find out. The second report of my study is now available. As well as that, I can arrange for you to see the video we took two weeks ago. Better still, why don't you join us as a visitor next week?

QUESTION 2 So how does all this qualify as research? You are not even registered at a university.

ANSWER No, I don't need to be. Perhaps your view of a legitimate researcher was valid for twenty years ago. There has been an increasing emphasis on the movement of teacher as researcher, particularly through the work of Lawrence Stenhouse and his followers. His famous phrase 'using research means doing research' (1979) said that I as a teacher am required to take the findings of research studies and test them out in my own classroom. If they fit my situation I may adapt them as seems appropriate. If they do not fit I am entitled to conduct my own research into my own educational situation, and develop an alternative theory based on my own experience, that is grounded in the reality of my own teaching and validated by consultation with others. By validation I mean that colleagues agree that my statements and supporting evidence are appropriate to the situation, that I intend to speak the truth, that I am authentic as a practitioner, and that I choose a style of language that we both share. These are points put forward by Jürgen Habermas (1979) as social criteria if I and my validating colleagues, and you and I, are to reach common understanding and agreement. (See Chapter 11.)

As a teacher–researcher, I do not need to be registered at a university. It is not necessary for me to read for a higher degree, although I may do so if I wish. My research, grounded in my class practice, is every bit as valid an educational study as those conducted by students registered at the academy.

QUESTION 3 What do you mean by 'valid'?

ANSWER My answer is expanded in Chapter 11, but briefly here I can say that I hope to demonstrate in practice that I can back up any claims I am prepared to make. These claims will be about an improvement in my class practice, my pupils' education, and my own understandings. Any theories I put forward will be grounded in practice; that is, we shall be able to discuss the actualities that make me think in the way that I do. The process of validation is when you and I can agree together that these theories are justified. Our dialogue is an important part of that process, for it causes us to think about justifications. I have to be extra-critical of my own conclusions in the face of your questions. Validation does not mean always reaching a consensus, but it does imply reaching a common understanding that will act as a basis for dialogue.

QUESTION 4 I am not happy about your insistence that your type of research is legitimate. I doubt that any universities would entertain the notion.

ANSWER Your doubts would have been well founded up to about ten to fifteen years ago. Since then many universities, polytechnics and other institutes have tutors, lecturers, professors who are sympathetic and enthusiastic for the principles of educational action research. I think, for example, of the Universities of Bath, Lancaster, East Anglia, Edinburgh – and particularly of Sheffield University (where Jean Rudduck is Professor of Education). Sheffield Polytechnic has an MEd course by action enquiry. Kingston Polytechnic, Manchester Polytechnic and Bath College of Higher Education are all offering higher degrees with an emphasis on the work of the reflexive practitioner.

QUESTION 5 So, if I am to take up a degree course at an institute for higher education, and if I am to adopt an action research methodology, I have to enrol at one of those institutes and no other?

ANSWER No, not at all. The tide is turning away from the insistence by universities on the strict control of educational knowledge to an understanding by teachers of their own practice – that is, a democratisation of research. This movement is active in most universities and institutes as well, although at the moment it is true to say that many powerful interest groups within the institutes themselves still resist the takeover. After all, it is a battle of ideas, a power struggle. But certainly the action research movement is becoming significant in universities and institutes all over the United Kingdom. If you wish to adopt an action research methodology at a university, you must first find a tutor who will understand this style of research, and accept you as a student. It is up to you to make enquiries at the individual universities, and go along and talk with them. Remember, you are the client, and current trends are towards client-centred research. You are entitled to expect a support strategy from your tutor which is appropriate to your needs. Do not accept a soft sell that persuades you to follow a predetermined taught course. Stand on your rights as a thinking practitioner. You have a responsibility to your own ideals to follow them through and convert them into reality.

QUESTION 6 Right. Let us talk about your claim to generalise from a sample of one. I think that is unreasonable. Certainly I will accept that you can draw generalisations from a sample of ten, twenty, a hundred. But you cannot seriously claim to be able to generalise from an individual.

ANSWER In principle, yes, I do. But I think we need to be much clearer about this talk of generalisation. Traditional research is concerned primarily about making predictions. It is based on the principles of botany, that you successfully compare one plant with another. Scientists who believe in this sort of predicted knowledge apply the theory to people. People will behave, they say, in such and such a way if they are placed in controlled situations. This applies equally to learning. So, depending on the stipulated conditions of learning, then a certain form of learned behaviour will be the product.

An action researcher does not see herself as a 'sample'. She has made a decision to understand the world from her own point of view as an individual claiming originality and exercising her own judgement, intending her understandings to be used by others if they wish. Whether or not her understandings and judgements have this potential can only be demonstrated in practice by other researchers showing that they are following her example and using in their own lives the forms of practice and understanding that she has developed. Rather than seeing the idea of generalisability as appropriate to a propositional form of discourse, that is, ideas that can be read on a page or made in statements without a context of reality, action researchers see generalisability in terms of shared forms of life.

Traditional research is all about scientific results which may be quantified, duplication of tests, replication of experiments, prediction of how the data will fall out. Action research is all about people explaining to themselves why they behave as they do, and enabling them to share this knowledge with others.

QUESTION 7 You mentioned the word 'scientific'. You say that you are being scientific, that your action research methodology is formative. I say it is *ad hoc*, misleading and terribly muddled. May we have some scientific rigour, please.

ANSWER Certainly. You are mistaken in saying that it is *ad hoc*. My action research methodology is formative, as well as democratic and supportive. It is also scientific, far from *ad hoc*. I take 'scientific' to mean 'principled action based on rational thought'. Perhaps you take 'scientific' to mean 'controlled'. The action of my enquiry is based on a clear logic and procedural analysis of educational systems. I form my hypotheses, and test them rigorously against the data. I draw my conclusions, and I hold these up to public scrutiny and debate. My units of appraisal (that is, what I am studying) are clearly identified, and my standards of judgement, the methods I use, are vigorously tested against and through the experience of others involved in the research. I would say that my research design is not only rigorously scientific, but that it emphasises the need for a public validation by individual researchers of their claim to know that they are improving the quality of education for themselves and for the people in their care. I am thinking, for example, of the work of Popper (1972), and of the words of Peter Medawar (1969) who says that we are 'telling a story which we invent and criticise and modify as we go along, so that it ends by being, as nearly as we can make it, a story about real life'.

QUESTION 8 When you said you were conducting an experiment, I expected you to have a control. You must have a control against which you can match your experimental group.

ANSWER When I use the word 'experiment' it does not mean to experiment on people. I intend rather to set up a novel situation and experiment with the situation in collaboration with other people.

Why must I have a control in the way positivists use a control? You are assuming that education may be studied by breaking it down into dependent and independent variables. You can control the variables and test the effects. Action researchers reject this approach. It is inappropriate to their enquiries of the form 'How can I/we improve the quality of education here?'. They use a disciplined form of enquiry where the researcher makes public his problem, imagines a solution, acts, evaluates and modifies his problem. He uses public criticism as a check against which to judge the validity of his accounts.

QUESTION 9 If you are a researcher you must have some claim to expertise in your field. Yet you say you are not an expert. Please clarify.

ANSWER I am not an expert in the way perhaps that you mean. Perhaps you are thinking of someone who has amassed a quantity of knowledge and skills, and has developed an expertise in applying them. This person is acknowledged to 'know' more than others. He follows the popular notion of knowledge as a commodity, like money or cake, and he has more of it than other people.

I am not an expert in this sense. I do not claim to know more about the practices of my colleagues than they do, but by the same token I do not expect them to claim to know more about my practice than I do. We have worked hard to make claims about our own educational practices, and our claims are valid and worthy of respect. Martin Buber (1947) speaks of the humility of the educator. We are humble, in that we approach our research with a sense of tension, that we do not know and need to find out; but as we proceed we develop confidence in our practice both as teachers and researchers.

I have no intention of dictating terms to others, but I am prepared to engage in discourse with you. For me to generate a general form of educational theory I need to help you to make explicit the tacit knowledge which underpins your competent practice. In this sense we need each other as competent professionals who are going to work collaboratively to try to improve practice and to develop our understanding of the process of improving practice. In my own research I am not doing research on other people. I am studying my own educational development as I attempt to improve the quality of education with my pupils.

QUESTION 10 You seem to be measuring the progress of your pupils. Yet I see no evidence of pre-tests or post-tests. How can you measure anything without specific scales?

ANSWER No, I am not measuring in that sense. That is a concept of traditional research which is interpreted through quantitative results. I am not measuring because I interpret my findings in qualitative terms rather than quantitative. If I feel that some tests would be useful indicators, then certainly I will use them. I do not reject any resources out of hand, but instead assess their potential and include them if they look promising. For example, some standardised reading tests can be very helpful, and attitudinal tests – but I will use the statistical results only as indicators for further research in an action research mode. As an action researcher I am seeking to explain and enhance, rather than only describe. Statistics-based tests will describe to me the situation as it is, without taking due account of the social and personal factors that make it so. They also stop at this point of description. It is my action research that will now lead me forward to apply the results in an effort to improve the quality of learning. I will incorporate such statistical devices into my overall research plan if I feel they have a contribution to make, but I would never regard them as a foundation.

So 'measuring' does not enter into the question. What I am doing is noting where the educational situation is now (what the children are doing and thinking, what my own practice is about), attempting to move it forward, and recording the intermediate action in an attempt to account for the movement forward. The 'scale' I apply, that is my standards of judgement, are those agreed by validators of the research and myself that progress has been made. For example, we will look at the evidence (audio or video tape, pen and paper), agree criteria that would indicate movement (that children are more articulate in their English lessons, that they have engaged more in active learning in physics, that there is a more democratic atmosphere in staff meetings, etc.) and point to specific instances to show those criteria in action (Susan and Belinda speak about their discussion to the class, whereas three weeks ago neither said a word in public; Simon shows how he discovered that air weighed something; Mrs Brown's voice of dissent was given a courteous hearing in Monday's staff meeting rather than drowned in a flood of groans). Those are the ways in which I as a researcher can make a claim to be the best judge of my own educational practice. I am not measuring in a conventional sense. I am testing and appraising, and, in collaboration with validating colleagues, judging whether or not I have made a contribution in enhancing the quality of education.

QUESTION 11 Yours is a subjective investigation. Your data, your sources, even your subjects, are chosen, perceived and interpreted by you. How can you claim objectivity?

ANSWER I agree that my original sources are subjective, as you say. I identified my own educational problems, I imagined my solutions, put them into practice and monitored them, and I reassessed the problem. However I was not alone. When I first identified the problems I talked extensively with sympathetic colleagues who promised support throughout the research. When I decided to implement the imagined solutions I told my class what I was hoping to do. I invited them to become researchers with me of their own practice. I monitored my practice and the movement of the children. I made regular progress reports to children, parents and colleagues a feature of the research. I invited the children's comments on their progress and how we could further enhance the learning situation (see questionnaire 10) and based my future action on their suggestions (see videotape 5).

I agree that my research is subjective. So is the research of the children, parents and colleagues. All together they accumulate, and through intersubjective criticism they increase their objectivity. Put simply another way: if I say 'It's cold tonight', my subjective opinion, and you say 'It's cold tonight', your subjective opinion, we both agree to our individual subjectivities and reach an objectively positive statement: 'It is cold tonight'. Action research involves other people, all applying their own personal, subjective knowledge in a critical way. If they all agree, then it is possible to claim objectivity.

However, objectivity is perhaps not a vital criterion. Does it matter if my research is subjective? I know what I know. In my opinion, the most vital knowledge for teachers is their intuitive, tacit knowledge. Michael Polanyi (1958, 1975) speaks of personal knowledge as being the most precious gift in the life of man. Perhaps a prime task of action research is to give to the idea of personal knowledge the esteem that it deserves, to encourage teachers to rely more on their tacit knowledge as the basis of a wise and considered practice. Often, when children are asked to give reasons why they think as they do, they will reply, 'I can't explain it. I just know.' Perhaps as teachers we ought not to try to defend our intuitive knowledge too hard, but give it objective status through intersubjective criticism.

QUESTION 12 Where does action research fit in with all the other activities a teacher carries out? Surely you aren't claiming it is an answer to all the problems we face from day to day in school?

ANSWER No, I am not. As with anything, there is a time and a place for action research. As far as I am concerned, the most important function of teachers is to create helping relationships, and to work towards establishing a warm, caring atmosphere that will encourage those relationships. I am against the idea of education as schooling. I am in favour of the idea of school being the place to help promote the autonomy and integrity of individuals. Whitehead also comments (1986): 'The majority of circumstances in education require warm and caring relationships to improve them. These qualities are often more important than the use of a systematic form of enquiry.'

However, the encouragement of these attitudes depends on the skills of the teacher. These skills are of a personal and social nature. Some people seem to have an intuitive knack of how to do it. For others it is not so easy. There is a great need (see Chapter 12) for the necessary in-service support to teachers to develop an appropriate kind of interpersonal expertise that will enable them to see education in the light of one-to-one relationships between caring persons, and that will help them to create those relationships.

A valuable contribution by action research to this approach to education is that it encourages a teacher to take careful stock of what is happening and how to improve the situation. In this sense it can be a useful diagnostic and evaluative tool. It will not in itself, however, teach specific competencies. It can help a teacher to home in on a problem and attempt solutions, but it cannot of itself open minds. The development of interpersonal skills needs specific support and guidance by the teachers of teachers. That in itself will assist teachers to decide if action research is a relevant strategy or if other approaches are more suitable.

QUESTION 13 Very well, I accept all you say as an indication of your honest endeavour. I will listen sympathetically to further explanations of action research, and perhaps I will try it out for myself. But I am still stuck on one crucial point. All these developments you point to have happened, but they may well have happened without you. They might have been in the pipeline already, and all your intervention may well have had nothing at all to do with it.

ANSWER True, but the point is that they ARE happening WITH me. Further, I can show you evidence on video and audiotape, on written records by pupils and participating colleagues, and by validation groups. I can say that the enhancement in the quality of this particular educational situation has come about because of my initial intervention as an action researcher. And then I will ask you to look at the action before the study and the action at present, and ask you to identify with me criteria of performance that we both agree will indicate the movement we speak of; and then point to critical moments throughout the evidence that are instances of those criteria in action. Together we will work towards a realisation in practice of our own educational enquiry in determining that my intervention was crucial. In this way, you and I become collaborators in our own educational enquiry. We observe our practice and we agree a joint theory between us of that practice.

In undertaking our separate enquiry we come back to your original sticking-point, that such improvements may well have happened without me. Consider: had you not challenged my ideas in the first place, had my action research study not existed to prompt you to ask these questions of me, would the enhancement in your own thinking have taken place? Would not you have remained in the same place as you were at the beginning of our discussion? As it is, you have become an active researcher, as have I. Even if you are not convinced of all that I have to say, you have listened, and our dialogue has sparked off new ideas in your mind. We have created through our dialogue new ideas and new beginnings.

# Chapter 11

# Claims to Validity

One of the problems associated with all kinds of research is that of validity, that is, does the research really do the things it claims to do, and are the results to be believed? There is a popular belief that the methods of a positivist approach are infallible, and that the results are unquestionably correct because they are usually objectivised and subjected to rigorous statistical analysis. It is supposed that because there is little human input to the data, the results are uncontaminated and reliable. The oversight in this way of thinking is that the data have to be analysed and interpreted by fallible people. Polanyi (1958) gives an excellent account of how such 'foolproof' results are sometimes badly misleading.

A common challenge to action research is that it is subjective and therefore unreliable, that is, the solutions that it claims to generate cannot be universally tested and are therefore invalid. Pam Lomax (1986) makes the point that

> as action researchers we do not claim to find the final answer to a question, but we do claim to improve (and change) educational practice through the educational development of practitioners. . . . The validity of what we claim would seem to be the degree to which it was useful (relevant) in guiding practice for particular teachers and its power to inform and precipitate debate about improving practice in the wider professional community.

There are three steps towards establishing the validity of a claim to knowledge. In the claim 'I know that I have improved the process of education for the students in my care' the implications are of (1) self validation, (2) peer validation and (3) learner validation.

## 1 Self validation

There are certain criteria which justify an individual's claim to knowledge. They include:

### (a) PRACTICE AS A REALISATION OF VALUES

An educational enquiry begins with a declaration, spoken, written or thought, of values: 'I believe that my children should be responsible for their own learning', for example. Often the enquiry comes into being because those values are being denied in practice. In this case the children are not responsible for their own learning, so something needs to be done about it. This is where the cycle of imagined solutions, implementation, observation, evaluation, re-planning is enacted. The desire to turn a negative state into a positive one, the motivation to improve education, acts as an incentive for the enquiry.

### (b) INTENTIONAL CRITICAL REFLECTION

'Critical reflection is the way in which a naive understanding of practice is transformed; where the practitioner reflects upon instead of merely experiencing practice; and where the process is made public and shared so that others gain an understanding of the practice' (Lomax, 1986). A claim to be able to explain one's own educational development depends on critical reflection, a desire to explore an intuitive understanding of practice and communicate it to others.

### (c) THE NEED FOR DISCIPLINED ENQUIRY

The series of questions on page 38 offers a common-sense procedure for pinpointing crucial stages in an enquiry. Although it is a very useful instrument in organising a plan of action, it must not be seen as the only way forward. Individual researchers may develop other schemes that they see as more appropriate to their own needs, such as the other schemes outlined in this book. What is important is that a researcher demonstrates publicly that he has followed a system of disciplined enquiry in arriving at his hypotheses.

### (d) PERSONAL INTERPRETATIONS AS A BASIS FOR DIALOGUE

The most underrated quality of teachers is their intuitive, tacit knowledge. In *Personal knowledge* (1958) Michael Polanyi's purpose was 'stripping away the mutilations which centuries of objectivist thought have imposed on the minds of men'. He pointed to the values of deep respect and commitment to anyone making a claim to personal knowledge:

> . . . Any conclusion, whether given as a surmise or claimed as a certainty, represents a commitment of the person who arrives at it. No one can utter more than a responsible commitment of his own, and this completely fulfils his responsibility for finding the truth and telling it. Whether or not it is the truth can be hazarded only by another, equally responsible commitment.

The strength of action research is that individual teachers interpret their own practice and make decisions about improving it. Their action is deliberate, based on the criteria discussed here. Self validation follows Polanyi's statement that 'I am a person claiming originality and exercising his personal judgement responsibly with universal intent'. The words here that need emphasising are 'universal intent'. The implication is that individuals recognise the potential in their interpretations of their own practice. Such personal judgements may make a significant contribution to the lives of other people. One individual, in making public his particular form of life, invites others to share that form. If others are prepared to do so, they agree that it is worthwhile, that is, they validate his way of life and his claim to knowledge. Two or more persons joining together along one particular chosen path indicate their agreement that that is a correct way for them.

## 2 Peer validation

Research findings are of social value only if they may be communicated to others. It is a central issue of action research to encourage teachers to make their intuitive knowledge public, by engaging in debate with others about their claims to know. 'I know that I have improved the process of education for myself and for the students in my care' may be valid for the individual practitioner; his claim must now be validated externally, by other people, who can also agree that his findings will be useful to their own practice.

Validation groups are part of the procedure of an action research enquiry. In research projects based at the University of Bath, we have used groups consisting of three to ten sympathetic individuals. They may be colleagues, advisers, parents, researchers – anyone who will be able to give a reasoned, critical assessment. Their task is to listen attentively to the individual teacher's claim to knowledge, consider the evidence, and agree that movement has or has not taken place. The evidence is often in the form of video recordings. The validation groups will critically assess the action with the researcher and agree criteria and examples in action that show the realisation of educational values through practice.

The task of the validation group is to help the researcher move his ideas forward. The atmosphere must be supportive, but challenging, encouraging the researcher to give responses to questions in the form of new questions for himself, protecting his emergent thinking, and giving him the confidence to act in a new direction.

The procedure for convening a validation group would be:

1 Well before the meeting, enclose a report of the research so far.
2 Ask the members to consider such questions as:
   Is the report a valid description of an educational process?
   Does the evidence support the claims that the researcher is making?
   Are there indications, critical moments, that show a living through of educational values?
3 View the evidence at the meeting, refer to the transcript of the tape if there is one, talk to the researcher about the report.

It will be necessary to hold several validation meetings at critical intervals in the research study.

The ethic of peer validation is to engage in dialogue; the method is question and answer. Jürgen Habermas has evolved a theory of social communication, which is very useful for action researchers. He has identified four characteristics which, if agreed by persons engaging in communication, he believes will ensure the validity of that communication. The criteria are:

(1) that a statement is TRUE;
(2) that the speech act is COMPREHENSIBLE;
(3) that the speaker is AUTHENTIC (sincere);
(4) that the situation is APPROPRIATE for these things to be said.

So, applied to my claim to knowledge, you and I must agree together that:

(1) what I say about my practice is true;
(2) that we both use words and expressions that we both understand;

(3) that we are both sincere and will avoid any deception;
(4) that the situation is right for us to be discussing this issue.

Dialogue has its meaning in the mutually dependent questions and answers of persons. The logic of question and answer is also known as dialectical logic. This logic is of particular interest to action researchers, because it stresses the need to find appropriate questions. Questions mean that the researcher is thinking critically about his practice (which is in fact a living form of previous answers); dialogue means that co-practitioners are engaging in a shared discourse. It is validation as a living form.

## 3 Learner validation

It is particularly useful to get on record the reactions of the clients themselves. Their evidence is perhaps the strongest support in the researcher's claim to knowledge. This may be presented in short written statements, diaries, or tape or video recordings.

John, for example, video recorded his class at the beginning of his research study to explore the development of moral values. The discussion centred around the group's reaction to hypothetical moral dilemmas. He took Kohlberg's famous example (1976) that Heinz's wife would die unless she received a certain drug that had just been manufactured by a local scientist. It was dreadfully expensive, an honest return for the years of labour that the scientist had invested. Was Heinz justified in stealing it?

The group responded in a lively, articulate manner.

> 'No, stealing is wrong under any circumstances.'
> 'But the scientist is wrong for charging so much.'
> 'His duty to his wife is greater than his duty to the scientist.'

At intervals during the study John video recorded the group engaging in similar discussions. Nine months after the first recording, he and his children viewed the series together, and John then made a recording of their reactions. They agreed that they had moved forward from their original stand, giving instances of their emergent thinking over the period of the study, and reasons for any changes in their thinking. John was then able to show this video to his peer validation group. This was a powerful chain of validation.

## Conclusion

In the final analysis, a claim to valid knowledge may be realised only through interaction. Habermas says (1976): 'In the interaction it will be shown in time whether the other side is "in truth or honestly" participating or is only pretending to engage in communicative action.'

The issue of validation reflects the strengths of action research; its relevance, emancipation, democracy and collaboration. Before any researcher may embark on helping to develop others' education, he must first develop his own; and he must honestly attempt to understand the processes and experiences, and share those understandings with others. It is only through self-knowledge that we may hope to know others, and it is only through a commitment to professional development that we can hope to improve the quality of education in our own classrooms.

# Chapter 12

# A Fresh Perspective on In-Service Support Through Action Research

1980s initiatives in in-service education have focused increasingly on school-based curriculum reform. There is a shift away from institutionalised taught courses which tend to look at issues of the management of schools and the curriculum to localised initiatives which identify particular needs of individual schools. What is urgently needed now is a further shift towards practitioner-centred research, not only in a political sense, that a view of the curriculum suggests that teachers should be afforded more status as professional educators, but also in a personally ideological sense, that teachers should be encouraged actively to view themselves as researchers of their own practice. There is a potentially two-directioned pressure here, one from 'external' policy makers, and the other from the individual practitioners themselves. This new emphasis would also encourage a move away from the idea of education as schooling and the management of systems towards a view of personalised client-centred attention.

There still seems to be a prevailing view through the in-service field that teachers are required to 'come up to standard'. Current discussions about accountability and appraisal, and an encroaching order of meritocracy go a long way towards underpinning these notions. National curriculum proposals (1987) specify: 'We must raise standards consistently . . . (and) . . . enable schools to be more accountable for the education they offer to their pupils' (pp. 2/3, 4).

There is much exhortation through the media for teachers to professionalise themselves and to improve their expertise. The consumer base to the philosophy of education is given further weighting by the national curriculum proposals in wanting strict controls on education.

> The division of responsibility for monitoring the delivery of the national curriculum in local authority-maintained schools between HMI and LEA inspectors will be the subject of further consultations with the local authority associations. Another essential part of the monitoring arrangements will be action by parents, who will be able to pinpoint deficiencies in the delivery of the national curriculum from the information about objectives and performance provided to them.
>
> (p. 23) (DES 1987)

To me, this is an amazingly naive view of professional assessment. The same innocence is reflected in proposals for blanket testing that suggests that all children perform in a uniform fashion, and that their progress along these set courses is a matter of correct input from their teachers.

There is a lack, particularly in these proposals, and also in our in-service provision in general, of a characterisation in practice of standards of expertise. So far the literature does not give detailed guidance about what appropriate standards appear to be, nor about how teachers should aim to reach those standards. Imprecise comments about coming up to standard are no use to teachers who have only their own intuitive knowledge to fall back on.

Denis Vincent (personal correspondence) points out that my allegation of vagueness and naivety in the consultative document on national curriculum palls into insignificance in the face of

> the huge new questions which have to be answered, starting with the role of the action researcher as an agent for change in a system which is in itself about to undergo radical (if not catastrophic?) change. How will this affect the role or agenda of a teacher researcher? What advice is now to be given to those who find themselves faced with an institutionalised denial of their educational values brought about by official legislation? An 'ideal' analysis would probably identify the main examples of categories of problem which will have to be faced and point to action research strategies for responding to them. For example, will the climate in some schools become less favourable towards professional extension of the sort argued for in this book? One particularly likely candidate problem is that teachers will be shackled to test-oriented programmes of work which they may

find narrow in conception. On a more positive side, there has been great emphasis on the teacher as diagnostician and there is some research evidence that this could be a highly problematic aspect of practice. How might a teacher respond to this challenge?

Such questions are at present unanswerable. To tackle them we need time to allow the shape and consequences of the Bill to become clearer.

Educational research needs to be grounded in a valid interpretation of what 'educational' means. Present trends towards examination-focused curricula and teacher accountability indicate that education emphasises the production of increased knowledge rather than an understanding of the development of persons. A swing towards the latter characterisation, an understanding of how people develop as autonomous individuals, would not deny, but rather enhance, pupils' ability to take on the necessary skills and competencies in order to function appropriately in society. A person-centred approach towards education and educational research would expedite their acquisition of the knowledge base of the curriculum. In this sense, practitioner-centred action research is a possible solution to some of the problems inherent in the proposed national curriculum.

Warm, caring relationships at the heart of education in schools provides an atmosphere that encourages children to be responsible for their own learning. Such relationships do not simply happen, but are arranged through the personal and interpersonal skills of committed, caring teachers. These skills in turn do not simply happen, but are the result of an attention to personal practice in which there is a supreme realisation of the value of persons.

A practitioner-centred approach to educational research equates personal research with a professionalisation of practice. Action research offers a fresh perspective on in-service education. There is not only the need for teachers to develop the professional skills and competencies of teaching, but also to develop a rationale for undertaking their own living form of enquiry, that is, to justify why they do as they do, and to be prepared to give instances of their coming-to-know (Stronach, 1986).

Such an approach to in-service education needs acknowledgement and vigorous support from teachers themselves, from the wider community, and from support agencies.

## Teachers' attitudes

Although the concept of practitioner-centred research has been around for some time now, it still needs to be popularised in schools. Walker makes the point (1985) that 'the question is not primarily one of maximising research design but of establishing enabling conditions. Consequently research is seen as interrelated with organisation, curriculum and teaching: it has an educational as well as a research purpose'. Tony Cassidy (in Hustler *et al.*, 1986) captures a predominant view with: 'Cynics may blame the anti-intellectual, anti-theoretical bias of many staffrooms, best characterized as "it's all very well for these researchers/lecturers/educationists, they don't have to take 4C last thing on a Friday".' Teachers need to be encouraged to see the value of classroom-based research, and to adopt a personal construct of themselves as researchers.

The talk about enhanced professional standards is appropriate to the idea of education for teachers, provided those standards are spelt out and examples given in practice. Those standards should be not only of technical teaching skills and competencies, but also of the personal and interpersonal variety. Teachers must take on board the need to professionalise themselves in all these aspects, in attempting to improve the quality of education for their pupils, and also in publicising their own deep understandings of how they have learnt and developed as teachers and as persons. In doing so, teachers set their own standards. They become self-accountable professionals, by being explicit about their own professional criteria, and by showing how they come to meet those criteria. The in-service revolution focuses on the need for practitioner-centred, practitioner-rationalised educational research. The two sides of the coin are an enhancement of the quality of education in terms of personal and social benefit for the clients, and an improvement in the quality of education in terms of understandings and explanations for the teacher. For this revolution to be effective, teachers must not be content to be taught, but endeavour to take on the responsibility of understanding for themselves.

## Attitudes of the wider community

Revolutions usually start small and take some time to make an impact. The idea of teachers being responsible for themselves will inevitably take time to penetrate all areas of the educational system. Stenhouse's message has been acknowledged since the 1970s, but the implications of his message are still not widely accepted. (It is interesting that Galileo's ideas were 'officially' accepted in 1985.)

It is important for teachers to be aware that they will meet turbulence if they become thinking practitioners. Action research is political in that its aim is to change, and change is bound to affect some part of the institution in which the research is located. Politics are about power, and power is often expressed in the domination of one will over another. The politics of educational knowledge are about the battle for ideas and values, establishing them through the literature (theoretical, propositional knowledge) and through the reality of schools and other institutions (practical, institutionalised knowledge).

For all sorts of reasons, groups who have a vested interest in the status quo will resist change vigorously and try to keep the system intact. This is true of most areas of change, and does not only apply to educational settings. Any innovations will set up counter-currents of opposition. When it is a question of the action of education, however, which is a value-saturated area, much turbulence is bound to start.

Volumes could be written about the life and death of genuinely useful projects by genuinely caring teachers. When one set of values comes into conflict with another, the struggle for power begins, perhaps the power of the institution against the individual, as well as the power of an established ideology against a new one.

*For example*:

Ray is very keen on modern technology. Having attended a course at his teachers' centre, he was anxious to introduce computer-assisted learning into his English lessons. The proposal was met with distinct disapproval, if not hostility, by his head of department. Her objections were that (a) the department did not have a computer of its own, (b) such funds as were available had already been allocated to books and other badly needed conventional resources, (c) no one else in the department was familiar with computers and the software available. Ray was not easily put off. He brought the matter up at the next departmental meeting, offering to teach colleagues how to use the technology, and to guide them in the choice and use of available software. He also pointed out that a computer could be made available through negotiation with other departments. The plan was met with enthusiasm by two colleagues, but not by two others, who shared the views of the head of department.

He declared his intentions of conducting his own enquiry, and his two colleagues agreed to collaborate. Over the next few weeks he negotiated the use of computer time with the business studies department and presented his case to the administrative deputy head for some timetable changes to enable his pilot class to engage in computer-assisted learning. He started keeping records in a rigorous fashion about his materials, the progress of his pupils, his conversations with his two colleagues about his practice and any changes in that practice and their reasons, the development of his own understandings.

He felt he had something to show for his efforts at the end of a term. He wrote a short report and presented it at the end of term English departmental meeting. His two supportive colleagues expressed their interest in following a similar project with some of their classes, and asked the head of department to represent them to the deputy head for the necessary re-timetabling. The head of department refused, saying that the study had gone ahead without general approval and that it was contrary to current departmental policy. Ray consulted the headmaster, who felt that he could not support Ray's requests.

There may be no answer to problems like Ray's in the short term. Long-term consolation may be found as the action research movement gains in momentum and credibility.

It is almost inevitable that a teacher wishing to take up an action enquiry will encounter some sort of resistance from someone. If she publicly announces that she intends to follow a disciplined enquiry and opts for an action research – or indeed any research – mode, she will probably encounter challenges for her changed practice as voiced in Chapter 10. It is difficult to meet such challenges and to sustain the determination to do something about an unsatisfactory situation if one feels alone and unsupported. This is when there is an urgent need for support from external agencies.

It is bound to take time for the wind of change to blow through the in-service field, and to change people's attitudes towards practitioner-centred research. The movement will gain in credibility the more attention is paid to it through the media, and the more teachers on the job are prepared to stand up and be counted as reflective practitioners.

## Attitudes of support agencies

The hope that teachers will become increasingly responsible for their own learning does not suggest a diminution in the amount of in-service support needed. If anything, that support should be increased, but the emphasis shifted to accommodate the changed perspective.

Until the 1980s, advisory and other support services usually kept a discreet distance from the classroom. It has always been normal practice for supervisors to go into class with trainees or probationers. Once that period of training and support was over, however, the new teacher was on her own, far removed from the carefully supportive atmosphere of the institute to the sometimes alien and sometimes frighteningly lonely confines of the classroom. It is an equivalent shock that many people experience when passing a driving test; a sense of freedom mixed with the anxiety of responsibility for one's own actions.

Advisory support in the classroom is mainly a 1980s innovation. Until recently such attendance in the classroom was viewed with suspicion, in fear that a teacher was being checked up on. The move towards practitioner-centred research is breaking down such barriers, and opening up a new debate between teachers and their supporters, with all parties' professional functions and areas of concern changing as a result of this discussion of practice.

There is a long way to go. Advisers from LEAs, senior school staff, consultants from the universities need to be persuaded of the need to help teachers in their own enquiries, and to provide systematic support and enthusiasm. There is an urgent need for such personnel to work with teachers on an intimate basis, not as supervisors but as collaborators. There is a need for them to encourage collaborative action research between colleagues in the same school and in clusters of schools, and to set up the necessary machinery to facilitate exchange of ideas and personnel; to encourage the setting up of networks and chains of communication; to ensure the necessary input of funds for equipment and ancillary personnel; to encourage teachers to write for a wider audience and take part in seminars and conferences; to be available to teachers as and when required.

All this supportive activity needs support itself. Quis custodiet . . .? Built into our educational system should be provision for the training of trainers, again, not on a hierarchical basis as in traditional patterns of in-service, but as a collaborative enquiry. In-service for in-service promises to be a central issue for the 1990s, and an area of the educational system that should be addressed immediately, but seems so far to have received little attention in the literature. The work that we are doing at Bath is attempting to answer a number of questions raised by individual practitioners in the in-service field.

Right across the in-service field there is a need for dialogue aimed at identifying and attempting to resolve problems of practice. Some networks are already in existence (see Chapter 13), but there is need for more. Such networks provide the frameworks of care that are essential for teachers to make their decision to exercise their right to change.

## Coping strategies

The content of this chapter so far looks mainly at future prospects. In the meantime, teachers have to get on with the business of today. Support is still limited, and teachers frequently find themselves on their own in a school when they decide to undertake their own action enquiry. There is often a tentative attitude towards them by colleagues, particularly when values conflict, and it takes a lot of courage and determination to carry on. The following hints might help.

1 DON'T GIVE UP. Courage and tenacity are needed in the ideas revolution.

2 ENLIST THE HELP OF COLLEAGUES. Talk to other colleagues who might be able to help. Talk to colleagues in school and further afield. Ask your headteacher for support. Ask her to put you in touch with a subject or INSET adviser. Get formal recognition for your project. If there is no provision now, try later.

3 KEEP A POSITIVE ATTITUDE. Do not be defensive. Do not take an aggressive stance that implies injured dignity or unfair treatment. Aim at dialogue, a two-way negotiation out of trouble.

4 BE PREPARED TO COMPROMISE. Action research is multi-directional; other people are involved, and if one party is expected to give ground, so must others.

5 BE GENEROUS. The task of researchers is to bring people together. They are strong persons. With a sure foundation they can afford to be generous and invite opponents to join with them in good spirit.

6 GO PUBLIC. Any action research will already have been announced to the community. In the face of opposition it is useful to become even more public. Find out potential supporters.

Invite them to become participants, and always leave the door open for opponents to join in as well. Produce more verbal and written reports, small ones rather than lengthy tomes which tend to be off-putting. Aim at establishing an action research network within the school or institution (see Chapter 13). People might be curious at your tenacity, but they will respect you and your project as being someone who believes in herself and her principles.

7 JOIN A LOCAL ACTION RESEARCH GROUP. If there is not one, form one. Aim to join professional associations such as BERA and attend their conferences (see Chapter 13, p. 150).

8 ESTABLISH A REPUTATION FOR SUCCESS. Let the findings of your research be known. Ask the children or other participants to be open about the fact that you have invited them to become co-researchers.

9 PUBLISH REPORTS IN JOURNALS. So you have never tried getting something published before? Everyone, including the most successful authors, had to start somewhere.

10 HAVE FAITH IN YOUR OWN PERSONAL KNOWLEDGE. At the end of the day, this is what counts. All the support on earth cannot substitute for quiet, unshakeable confidence in yourself. Be sure of yourself as a rational, committed person, who is as entitled to her place on this earth as any other. For it is not on technological or economic power that the future of this planet depends, but on the firm, intent commitment of caring, purposeful teachers to improve the quality of education, here and now.

# Chapter 13

# Widening the Network

## Networks

Although there are several initiatives going on in the United Kingdom to establish regional and national networks, there is as yet only one thriving network, based at Cambridge. This is CARN, the Classroom Action Research Network. This is a national and international network of action researchers which arose out of the Ford Teaching Project in 1975.

CARN publishes bulletins to which practising educationalists are invited to contribute, and it organises conferences and seminars. A 1987 initiative has been the foundation of regional networks headed by coordinators who organise the names and interests of members for the CARN Directory. This membership list and other information is available from the overall coordinator, Bridget Somekh.

Contact: Bridget Somekh,
Unit for Educational Development,
School of Education,
University of East Anglia,
Norwich. NR4 7TJ

In Northern Ireland there is an active Teacher Research Network which has an annual conference and publishes an annual Bulletin.

Contact: Barry Hutchinson,
University of Ulster,
Coleraine,
Co. Londonderry.

## Regional initiatives

Many authorities see the need for area networks, and are keen to support such initiatives. For example, as part of the Avon Curriculum Review and Evaluation Programme, the coordinators, Terry Hewitt and Gill Watson, put out a newsletter of which the following is a section:

> In 1986–87 teachers from 11 Avon schools were involved in classroom focussed enquiries as part of a curriculum review and evaluation initiative, receiving support and funding through TRIST. The focus was on the classroom experience of young people and the classroom strategies adopted by their teachers. The approach used was a systematic form of 'action enquiry' in which activities focussed on the quality of education in the classroom.
>
> Action enquiry is a form of enquiry which traces the following route:
>
> Stage 1: Discuss your concern(s) – what are you wanting to improve?
> Stage 2: Decide on a strategy for change and improvement.
> Stage 3: Put that strategy into effect – ACT!
> Stage 4: Evaluate the outcomes of your actions.
> Stage 5: Modify your 'statement of concern' in the light of this evaluation.
>
> School-based work was supported by workshops and by dialogue between teacher colleagues and professional 'supporters' from outside the school who helped reflect problematic classroom practice back to the school's own teacher researchers. Evaluation reports submitted by each of the participating schools provided some evidence that classroom-based research is part of a collaborative commitment to improve the quality of education. There was 'ample evidence from this programme that teachers enthusiastically welcome this type of support and see it as distinctly preferable to many of the INSET opportunities they have traditionally been offered'.
>
> Following the authority's decision to make a funding allocation for the continuation of this type of teacher support the structure of Avon's curriculum review and evaluation programme has been

> established. The model that has been adopted is to support the classroom research of six groups of teachers, three of whom were involved in TRIST 1.3 and three who are new to this kind of in-service work. Terry Hewitt and Gill Watson have been appointed coordinators; one of them will be at RLDU each Thursday afternoon to deal with telephone or personal enquiries.

The letter goes on to list the schools involved, and finishes:

> If other schools are already involved in this type of enquiry we would be pleased to hear about their work. It is hoped that this newsletter may help develop the network of expertise.

## Professional centres

Most teachers' centres or other professional centres are happy to be the focus of a local action research group. The initiative for forming such a group usually comes from an individual or a small group of teachers who circulate to colleagues, inviting them to form such a group. The steps for doing so might include:

1. Circulate to all schools in the designated area through the pages of the teachers' centre term programme, or a specially prepared information sheet. Explain clearly what the aim is, and invite colleagues to a preliminary meeting to discuss the proposal.
2. Have a specific input at this meeting. It is cosy to meet informally, but there is a need for teachers to see that there is a point to the action and that it will be sustained to their advantage. Teachers under pressure of time and work need to be persuaded to give up an evening for this preliminary meeting, and need to see the benefits to them in order to sustain a commitment. If possible, provide a person who is known to have something useful to say – a senior adviser, perhaps, or a person mentioned in this book. At the same time, make it clear that such a person is there in a support role. The main focus of the project is the teachers themselves.
3. Follow up this preliminary meeting with a planned programme. Involve the participants immediately. Perhaps arrange for three members to speak of their class practice at the next meeting – ten minutes each, say, with time for follow-up discussion. Or have a questionnaire ready to get feedback on how the teachers see the

future of this group. Do they want to identify particular issues that are relevant to them? Do they want to arrange visits to each other's schools? Do they need support agents to help them in their own enquiries?

4 Aim to set up a county or area network. Involve the senior INSET adviser or principal adviser. Try to arrange with him to set up local groups which will keep in close touch with each other. Arrange seminars and conferences on an area level to let people know what is going on and sustain enthusiasm. Sounds like hard work? It is, but it is worth the effort.

5 Get involved with action researchers on a wider basis. Aim to feed into the national networks. Attend conferences and contribute to the journals. Invite individuals from these groups to your own. Action research aims to set up communities of educational enquirers, but it all takes effort and dedication.

## School groups

Set up a school group of action researchers. Even two or three will form a recognised group. Get the support of senior colleagues and involve the appropriate advisers. Follow the same procedure as for professional centres, and do not be dissuaded by the fact that yours is only a small, local group. In this venture, every single individual is important; the movement starts with the individual, and grows to involve other individuals. Make the group's presence known in the school; ask for time at staff meetings, say, or publish a bulletin to keep others informed of your activities. Create a reputation for success which will then generate further success.

## Publications

Go public. Write up accounts of your own classroom research, or the activities of your group. Be bold in submitting to top journals. The mood is right for client-centred research, and editors are always looking for common-sense pieces which will have a wide appeal. Search the educational press for publications which you think might suit your purposes.

## British Educational Research Association

Join this association. There is an annual conference which provides a forum for teacher–researchers to present their own work to a critically supportive audience, as well as regional conferences which aim to strengthen the inquiry network. An annual subscription will bring you bulletins and updates on the movement.

Further information from: British Educational Research Association
Scottish Council for Research in Education
15 St. John Street
Edinburgh
Scotland
EH8 8GR

## Support for in-service supporters

The action research movement is growing very quickly. I have indicated at various places in the text that the movement is being adopted by the institutions as an in-service resource; in universities, polytechnics, institutes of initial teacher education, teachers' centres, schools and individual classrooms. More and more people are welcoming the innovation as a way of improving educational practice.

During the preparation of this book I contacted a number of action researchers who are interested in in-service provision. It seems to me and to a number of these colleagues that there should be a component within the national networks that provides support for the supporters. Perhaps this question should be addressed by the British Educational Research Association or similar body. The more the movement spreads, the more intense will be the need to provide liaisons and interlinks for the professional supporters of teachers who are engaged in their own action research enquiries. This issue is of particular importance in the face of the increased control of educational knowledge that is threatened for the 1990s.

I hope this idea is taken up in the literature and in the network conferences. For my part, I feel strongly that it is up to us all, individually and collectively, to do what we can within our own location to express our enthusiasm and determination to improve the quality of education for ourselves and for the people in our care.

## People to contact

The following people associated with this book would welcome comments.

Martin Forrest,
Department of Education,
Bristol Polytechnic,
Redlands Hill,
Bristol. BS6 6UZ

Jack Whitehead,
The School of Education,
University of Bath,
Claverton Down,
Bath. BA2 7AY

Jean McNiff,
c/o Macmillan Assessment,
Houndmills,
Basingstoke,
Hants.
RG21 2XS

# Bibliography


Adelman, C. and Young, M., 'The assumptions of educational research: the last twenty years in Great Britain' in Shipman, M. (ed) *Educational research: principles, policies and practices* (Falmer Press, 1985).

Atkinson, P. and Delamont, S., 'Bread and dreams or bread and circuses?' in Shipman, M. (ed) *Educational research: principles, policies and practices* (Falmer Press, 1985).

Aristotle, *Nichomachean Ethics* tr. H. G. Greenwood, (N.Y., Arno Press 1973).

Armstrong, M., *Closely observed children* (Writers and Readers, 1980).

Avon LEA, *In touch with the past – a practical approach to primary history* (Bristol, County of Avon, 1982).

Baldwin, J. and Wells, H., *Active Tutorial Work. Years 1 and 2; Years 3, 4 and 5; 6th Form* (Basil Blackwell, 1979–81).

Bassey, M., 'Does action research require sophisticated methods?' in Hustler *et al.* (eds) *Action research in classrooms and schools* (Allen and Unwin, 1986).

Bernstein, R., *Beyond objectivity and relativity; science, hermeneutics and praxis* (Basil Blackwell, 1983).

Buber, M., *The knowledge of man* (Allen and Unwin, 1965).

Buber, M., *Between man and man* (Fontana, 1947).

Burgess, R., (ed), *Field methods in the study of education* (Falmer Press, 1985).

Burgess, R. (ed), *Issues in qualitative research* (Falmer Press, 1986).

Button, L., *Developmental group work with adolescents* (Hodder and Stoughton, 1974).

Button, L., *Group tutoring for the form teacher* (Hodder and Stoughton, 1981).

Carr, W. and Kemmis, S., *Becoming critical: education, knowledge and action research* (Falmer Press, 1986).

Cassidy, T., 'Initiating and encouraging action research in comprehensive schools' in Hustler *et al.*, *Action research in classrooms and schools* (Allen and Unwin, 1986).

Chomsky, N., *Syntactic structures* (MIT, 1957).

Chomsky, N., *Aspects of the theory of syntax* (MIT, 1965).

Corey, S., *Action research to improve school practices* (N.Y., Columbia University, 1953).

Department of Education and Science, *The school curriculum*, Circular 6/81 (1981).

Department of Education and Science, *The National Curriculum 5–16: a consultation document* (1987).

Eames, K., *The growth of a teacher's attempt to understand writing, re-drafting, learning and autonomy in the examination years* (Unpub. M.Phil., University of Bath, 1987).

Ebbutt, D., *Teachers as researchers: how four teachers co-ordinate action research in their respective schools*, mimeo (Cambridge Institute of Education, 1982).

Ebbutt, D., *Educational action research: some general concerns and specific quibbles*, mimeo (Cambridge Institute of Education, 1983).
Also reprinted in Burgess, R. (ed) *Issues in educational research* (Falmer Press, 1985).

Ebbutt, D. and Elliott, J., *Issues in teaching for understanding* (Longmans, for Schools Council, 1985).

Elliott, J., *Action research; framework for self evaluation in schools*, TIQL working paper No. 1, mimeo (Cambridge Institute of Education, 1981).

Elliott, J. and Adelman, C., *Innovation at the classroom level: a case study of the Ford Teaching Project*, Unit 28, Open University Course E203: Curriculum Design and Development (Open University Press, 1976).

Elliott, J. and Adelman, C., 'Reflecting where the action is: the design of the Ford Teaching Project', *Education for teaching*, Vol. 92 (1973).

Fromm, E., *To have or to be* (Jonathan Cape, 1978).

Gadamer, H. G., *Truth and method* (N.Y., Seabury Press, 1965).

Gagné, R., *The conditions of learning* (Holt, Rinehart and Winston, 1965).

Glaser, B. and Strauss, A., *The discovery of grounded theory* (N.Y., Aldine, 1967).

Green, B., 'The theory practice problem seen from a classroom commitment to improve art education', *Journal of the National Society for art education*, Vol. 7 (1980).

Habermas, J., *Knowledge and human interests*, tr. J. J. Shapiro (Heinemann, 1972).

Habermas, J., *Communication and the evolution of society*, tr. T. McCarthy (Boston, Beacon Press, 1979).

Hamilton, D., 'Some contrasting assumptions about case study research and survey analysis' in Simons, H. (ed) *Towards a science of the singular* (Norwich, CARE, 1980).

Hirst, P., 'Educational theory' in Tibble, J. W. (ed) *The study of education* (Routledge and Kegan Paul, 1966).

Hirst, P., 'Human movement, knowledge and education', *Journal of the philosophy of education*, Vol. 13 (1979).

Hirst, P. (ed), *Educational theory and its foundation disciplines* (Routledge and Kegan Paul, 1983).

Hirst, P. and Peters, R., *The logic of education* (Routledge and Kegan Paul, 1970).

Hopkins, D., *A teacher's guide to classroom research* (Open University Press, 1985).

Husen, T. and Postlethwaite, T. (eds), *International encyclopedia of education: research and studies* (Pergamon, 1982).

Hustler, D., Bassey, M. and Cassidy, T., *Action research in classrooms and schools* (Allen and Unwin, 1986).

Jensen, M., *A creative approach to the teaching of English in the examination years: an action research project* (Unpub. M.Phil., University of Bath, 1987).

Kemmis, S., 'Action research' in Husen, T. and Postlethwaite T. (eds), *International encyclopedia of education: research and studies* (Pergamon, 1982).

Kemmis, S. and McTaggart, R., *The action research planner* (Geelong, Victoria, Deakin University Press, 1982).

Kohlberg. L., 'Moral stages and moralization: the cognitive developmental approach' in Lickona, T. (ed) *Moral development and behavior: theory, research and social issues* (N.Y., Holt, Rinehart and Winston, 1976).

Kohlberg, L., *Essays on moral development. Vol. 1. The philosophy of moral development* (San Francisco, Calif., Harper and Row, 1981).

Kuhn, T., *The structure of scientific revolutions* (University of Chicago Press, 1962).

Larter, A., *An action research approach to classroom discussion in the examination years* (Unpub. M.Phil., University of Bath, 1987).

Levi-Strauss, C., *Structural anthropology: Vol. 2* (Penguin, 1968).
Lewin, K., 'Action research and minority problems', *Journal of social issues*, Vol. 2 (1946).
Likona, T. (ed), *Moral development and behaviour: Theory, research and social issues* (N.Y., Holt, Rinehart and Winston, 1976).
Lomax, P., 'Evaluating for course improvement', *Assessment and evaluation in higher education*, 10, pp. 254–264 (1985).
Lomax, P., 'Action researchers' action research: a symposium', *British Journal of In-service Education*, 13 (1) pp. 42–50 (1986).
Lomax, P. and Whitehead, J., 'Action research and the politics of educational knowledge', *British Educational Research Journal* (1987).
Mager, R., *Preparing instructional objectives* (Palo Alto, Ca., Fearon, 1962).
Macdonald, B. and Walker, R (eds), *Innovation, evaluation research and the problem of control* (Norwich School of Education, University of East Anglia Press, 1974).
McGuire J. and Priestley, P., *Life after school: a social skills curriculum* (Pergamon, 1981).
McNiff, J., 'Action research: a generative model for in-service support', *British Journal of In-Service Education*, Summer (1984).
McNiff, J., *Personal and social education: a teacher's handbook* (CRAC: Hobsons, 1986).
McNiff, J., *An individual's claim to know her own personal and social development through the dialectic of action research* (Unpub. Ph.D. submission, University of Bath, 1988).
Medawar, P., *Induction and intuition in scientific thought* (Methuen, 1969).
Nias, J., *A more distant drummer: teacher developments as development of self* (Cambridge Institute of Education, 1984).
O'Connor, D., *An introduction to the philosophy of education* (Routledge and Kegan Paul, 1957).
Parlett, M. and Hamilton, D., 'Evaluation as illumination: a new approach to the study of innovatory programmes' in Tawney, D. A. (ed) *Curriculum evaluation today: trends and implications* (Macmillan Education, 1976).
Parlett, M. and Hamilton, D. (eds), *Beyond the numbers game* (Macmillan, 1977).
Peters, R., *Ethics and education* (Allen and Unwin, 1966).
Peters, R., *Education and the education of teachers* (Routledge and Kegan Paul, 1977).
Pike, K. L., *Language in relation to a unified theory of human behavior* (The Hague, Mouton, 1967).
Polanyi, M., *Personal knowledge* (Routledge and Kegan Paul, 1958).

Polanyi, M. and Prosch, H., *Meaning* (University of Chicago Press, 1975).

Popper, K., *Objective knowledge* (Oxford University Press, 1972).

Pring, R., *Personal and social education in the curriculum* (Hodder and Stoughton, 1984).

Rapoport, R., 'Three dilemmas in action research', *Human relations*, Vol. 23 (1970).

Reason, P. and Rowan, J., *Human Inquiry* (Wiley, 1981).

Revans, R. W., *Action learning* (Blond and Briggs, 1980).

Rowland, S., *The enquiring classroom: an introduction to children's learning* (Falmer, 1984).

Rudduck, J. (ed), *Teachers in partnership: four studies of inservice collaboration* (Longman, 1982).

Rudduck, J., *Making the most of the short inservice course* (Methuen, 1981).

Rudduck, J. and Hopkins, D. (eds), *Research as a basis for teaching* (Heinemann, 1985).

Sanford, N., 'Whatever happened to action research?', *Journal of social issues*, Vol. 26. (1970). Reprinted in Kemmis, S. *et al.* (eds) 'The action research reader' (Geelong, Victoria, Deakin University Press, 1982).

Schutz, A., *The phenomenology of the social world* (Evanston, Northwestern University Press, 1972).

Schwab, J. J., 'The practical: A language for curriculum' *School review* Vol. 78 (1969).

Shipman, M., *Educational research: principles, policies and practices* (Falmer Press, 1985).

Simons, H. (ed), *Towards a science of the singular* (Norwich, CARE, University of East Anglia, 1980).

Skilbeck, M., 'Lawrence Stenhouse: research methodology – "Research is systematic enquiry made public"', *British Educational Research Journal*, 9 (1), 11–20 (1983).

Skinner, B. F., *The technology of teaching* (N.Y., Prentice Hall, 1968).

Stake, R., 'The case study method in social enquiry' in Simons, H. *Towards a science of the singular* (Norwich, CARE, University of East Anglia, 1980).

Stenhouse, L., *Introduction to curriculum research and development* (Heinemann Education, 1975).

Stenhouse, L., 'Using research means doing research' in Dahl, H. *et al.* (eds) *Spotlight on educational research* (Oslo, University Press, 1979).

Stenhouse, L., Site lecture presented at Simon Fraser University, Vancouver 8/1980 quoted in Skilbeck, M. 'Lawrence Stenhouse: research methodology – "Research is systematic enquiry made public"', *British Educational Research Journal* 9 (1) 11–20 (1983).

Stronach, I., *Raising educational questions*, mimeo (Cambridge Institute of Education, 1986).

Tawney, D. A. (ed), 'Curriculum evaluation today: trends and implications' (Macmillan Education, 1976).

Torbert, W., 'Why has educational research been so uneducational?' in Reason, P. and Rowan, J. (eds) *Human Inquiry* (Wiley, 1981).

Walker, R., *The observational work of LEA inspectors and advisers* (Norwich, CARE, University of East Anglia, 1982).

Walker, R., *Doing research* (Methuen, 1985).

Warnock, M., *Schools of thought* (Faber and Faber, 1977).

Whitehead, J., 'The process of improving education within schools' Paper to the British Educational Research Association annual conference (1977).

Whitehead, J., 'An analysis of an individual's educational development: the basis for personally oriented action research' in Shipman, M. (ed) *Educational research: principles, policies and practices* (1985).

Whitehead, J., 'Action research and the politics of educational knowledge', *British Educational Research Journal* Vol. 13, No. 2 (1987).

Whitehead, J. and Barrett, J., 'Supporting teachers in their classroom research'. A collection of papers produced by Values in Education – a group of educational researchers in the School of Education, University of Bath (1985).

Whitehead, J. and Foster, D., 'Action research and professional development' Cambridge Action Research Network Bulletin No. 6 (1984).

Whitehead, J. 'In-service education as collaborative action research', *British Journal of In-service Education*, Vol. 13, No. 3, pp. 142–149 (1987).

# Index